ACHIEVING
EYPS

Teamwork and Collaboration in Early Years Settings

MARY STACEY

Series editors: Gill Goodliff and Lyn Trodd

LearningMatters

First published in 2009 by Learning Matters Ltd

British Library Cataloguing in Publication Data
A CIP record for this book is available from the British Library.

ISBN: 978 1 84445 267 5

Text design by Code 5 Design Associates Ltd
Cover design by Phil Barker
Project management by Swales & Willis
Typeset by Kelly Gray
Printed and bound in Great Britain by TJ International Ltd, Padstow, Cornwall

Learning Matters Ltd
33 Southernhay East
Exeter EX1 1 NX
Tel: 01392 215560
info@learningmatters.co.uk
www.learningmatters.co.uk

Contents

Foreword from the series editors

This book is one of a series which will be of interest to all those following pathways towards achieving Early Years Professional Status (EYPS). This includes students on Sector-Endorsed Foundation Degree in Early Years programmes and undergraduate Early Childhood Studies degree courses as these awards are key routes towards EYPS.

The graduate EYP role was created as a key strategy in government commitment to improve the quality of Early Years care and education in England, especially in the private, voluntary and independent sectors. Policy documents and legislation such as *Every Child Matters: Change for Children*, DfES (2004); the *Ten Year Childcare Strategy: Choice for Parents – the Best Start for Children*, HMT (2004), and the Childcare Act, 2006, identified the need for high-quality, well-trained and educated professionals to work with the youngest children. The Government's aim – restated in the 2020 Children and Young People's Workforce Strategy (DCSF, 2008) – is to have an Early Years Professional (EYP) in all children's centres by 2010 and in every full day care setting by 2015, with two graduates in disadvantaged areas.

In *Teamwork and Collaboration* Mary Stacey draws on her extensive experience as a trainer and facilitator with early years practitioners to focus on the EYP's professional relationships with other adults and in particular their role as an enabler within a team of colleagues.

Written essentially as a practical tool for early years practitioners, the author draws on theoretical perspectives and research studies to discuss and explore the concepts of 'teams', 'teamworking' and 'professionalism' within the government's intention to create an integrated, multi-disciplinary workforce. Throughout the book authentic case studies and practical tasks challenge the reader to reflect on their own values, beliefs and practice and to consider how professional learning is developed through communities of practice.

Teamwork and Collaboration will support candidates on any of the pathways towards achieving Early Years Professional Status and is likely to be a valuable source of training material for Continuing Professional Development through EYP Networks. We are delighted to commend it to you.

May 2009

Gill Goodliff   Lyn Trodd
The Open University   University of Hertfordshire

Acknowledgements

First I would like to thank the many early years practitioners that I have met over the past years. Ostensibly, I have been invited in to support them as they develop new practices or look at how to improve communication within their setting. But, as we have gone on a journey together, discussing ideas and wrestling with predicaments, they have offered me many new insights into ways of working and collaborating as teams in order to improve services for children, parents and the community.

While writing this book, I interviewed a number of early years practitioners in different parts of the country and in a variety of settings. Special thanks go to them; I appreciated their honesty and humour as they talked about their experiences taking on new roles and working in teams. I would also like to acknowledge their enthusiasm and commitment to creating an effective multi-agency service for children and their families, as they translate the policy into realistic practice, sometimes starting with small but significant steps.

My thanks to Julia Morris at Learning Matters and to Jennifer Clark for their help and comments through the different stages of writing. Finally, very many thanks to Gill Goodliff and Lyn Trodd, particularly Gill who encouraged me to write the book in the first place. She has listened carefully to my ideas, explored these with me through regular discussions and constantly given useful and practical feedback.

Mary Stacey

About the author and series editors

Mary Stacey

Mary Stacey is an independent training consultant with a background in early years teaching and community work with parents and young children. She is also a qualified assertiveness trainer. She has extensive experience working with practitioners, from a range of early years settings, on issues such as teamwork, managing change and developing new roles. Her past publications include books on establishing home-school relations and on developing skills for training. An academic consultant for the Open University, Mary has contributed to courses in the Foundation Degree in Early Years and accredited courses for Teaching Assistants.

Gill Goodliff

Gill Goodliff is a Senior Lecturer and Head of Awards for Early Years at the Open University where she has developed and chaired courses on the Sector-Endorsed Foundation Degree and been involved as a Lead Assessor for Early Years Professional Status. Gill's professional work with young children and their families was predominantly in the voluntary sector. Her research interests centre on the professional identities of Early Years practitioners and young children's spirituality.

Lynn Trodd

Lyn Trodd is Head of Children's Workforce Development at the University of Hertfordshire. Lyn is the Chair of the National Network of Sector-Endorsed Foundation Degrees in Early Years. She was involved in the design of Early Years Professional Status and helped to pilot the Validation Pathway when it first became available. Lyn has published and edited a range of articles, national and international conference papers and books focusing on self-efficacy in the child and the practitioner, and also the professional identity and role of adults who work with young children.

1   Setting the scene: the Early Years Professional within the team

C H A P T E R   O B J E C T I V E S

This book is primarily for those wishing to achieve graduate Early Years Professional Status (EYPS) but it is also relevant for anyone, whatever the stage in their professional training, who is a member of an Early Years team and wants to reflect on their role within it.

This chapter provides an overall framework for the book and identifies the relevant Early Years Professional (EYP) Standards for Teamwork and Collaboration (Standards 33–36) that have to be demonstrated for the award. It discusses how the role of the EYP has evolved as a result of government initiatives. It exemplifies the kind of settings that Early Years practitioners may work in and looks at the role an EYP may have within a team.

After reading this chapter you should be able to:
- identify the EYP Standards that apply to teamwork and collaboration;
- compare your setting and your role within it to other models described;
- reflect on the role of the EYP and the multi-layered meanings that underlie the title.

The Standards

The main focus of the book is on your relationships with other adults, particularly your colleagues, and on your role as enabler within a team. In the *Guidance to the Standards* for the award, the group of Standards for Teamwork and Collaboration (S33–S36) are described as follows:

> . . . these Standards do not relate to personal practice with young children, which practice is covered by all the other Standards; nor do they relate to managerial responsibilities, which fall outside the remit of the Standards for EYPS. They relate to EYPs' personal practice with colleagues, through which they provide leadership and support.
>
> (Children's Workforce Development Council (CWDC), 2008a, page 61)

Nevertheless, the children and families are the essential reason for developing good relationships with your colleagues and will be at the heart of your communications. As an EYP, you are likely to take the lead, and indeed are expected to demonstrate this through your practice, but your role as a team member is crucial too. For a full discussion on your role as leader, you can refer to Whalley, (2008) *Leading practice in early years settings*, which is also part of this series.

In the Standards for Teamwork and Collaboration, candidates for the EYPS must demonstrate their ability to:

- *S33*: establish and sustain a culture of collaborative and co-operative working between colleagues;

- *S34*: ensure that colleagues working with them understand their role and are involved appropriately in helping children to meet planned objectives;

- *S35*: influence and shape the policies and practices of the setting and share in collective responsibility for their implementation;

- *S36*: contribute to the work of a multiprofessional team and, where appropriate, co-ordinate and implement agreed programmes and interventions on a day-to-day basis.

These Standards cannot be discussed in isolation however, and will only be demonstrated in conjunction with those from the other groups of Standards. For example, you will need to demonstrate to your team your knowledge and understanding of the Early Years Foundation Stage and how to put this into practice (Standard 1), discussing and agreeing with them high expectations for children in their learning and development (Standards 7–24). You will also be supporting others in developing respectful and listening relationships with children (Standards 25–28) and engaging families and parents in meaningful partnerships (Standards 29–32). Hand-in-hand with this goes your own professional development (Standards 37–39).

The content

This is first and foremost a practical guide. It asks you to reflect on yourself and the groups you belong to, and on ways of collaborating and communicating more effectively. As a team member, you cannot work in isolation and some of the reflective tasks are designed for use with other members of a team. A number of the exercises you will encounter in this book have been used in a range of Early Years settings and many of the ideas come as a result of my work with practitioners. The case studies are based on my discussions and interviews with practitioners working across the Early Years sector. Names and, in some cases, the specific details have been changed to maintain the anonymity of individuals and settings. Each chapter includes references to theoretical perspectives and arguments related to this subject. As it is impossible in this book to include everything that has been written on such a complex area, you will find suggestions for further recommended reading at the end of each chapter.

As the *Guidance to the Standards* (CWDC, 2008a) points out, settings will vary and therefore affect the way you demonstrate your support and leadership within a team. You may be new to Early Years work and have worked elsewhere, but whatever your background, you will bring transferable skills and knowledge that can be shared with others who may bring something different from you. Thus in Chapter 2, we look at teams in general and how they develop, and then consider the framework required for them to work successfully. The *Guidance to the Standards* (CWDC, 2008a, page 63) suggests several ways of demonstrating this group of Standards from one-to-one meetings with colleagues, leading workshops or discussing ways of incorporating policy or changing practice. As an EYP you will need to be able to communicate well with your colleagues, particularly if asking for change.

In Chapter 4, we look at the ways personal interaction affects a team and discuss some strategies for communicating assertively. Collaboration is another skill you will need and in Chapter 5 we look at this in its fullest sense, suggesting some practical ways for creating forums where practitioners feel confident to discuss differences or ask questions. With the intention of raising quality across all settings, the Early Years Foundation Stage (EYFS) (Department for Children, Schools and Families (DCSF), 2008b) framework has required Early Years teams to re-evaluate their practice. And with the introduction and development of policy and legislation following the *Every Child Matters* Green Paper (Department for Education and Skills (DfES), 2003) and subsequent Children Act (2004) and Childcare Act (2006), many practitioners have experienced radical changes as services have joined up and roles and responsibilities have altered. In Chapter 7, we look at some of the debates concerning what developing a professional workforce entails and how you manage your own and your colleagues' anxiety and handle possible conflict in times of change. Picking up the themes of previous chapters, we end the book considering each within the broad context of a multi-agency team, and focus on the challenges of sharing information for the benefit of children and their families.

A children and young people's integrated workforce

Change is a feature of Early Years practice. If you have been working in Early Years for any length of time, you will be aware of the new policies and government initiatives impacting on the sector. One of the key areas that will have a continuing effect on the way you work with others is the way the children's workforce is expected to work in an integrated way. The *Common Core of Skills and Knowledge* (DfES, 2005a), often referred to as The Common Core, sets out the basic skills and knowledge needed by any workers, paid or voluntary, involved in regular contact with children, young people and families. There are six main areas that all practitioners are expected to fulfil in their work:

- effective communication and engagement with children, young people and families;
- child and young person development;
- safeguarding and promoting the welfare of the child;
- supporting transitions;
- multi-agency working;
- sharing information.

The Common Core is used for job descriptions, in induction, and in the development of training and professional qualifications across services for children and young people. It is also intended as a base for an Integrated Qualifications Framework so as to allow more opportunities for training and more mobility within the workforce. The *Children's Workforce Strategy* (DfES, 2005b, page 29) states that the reason that 40 per cent of practitioners are not qualified to Level 2, the basic level of training, has been the *lack of a framework clearly linking skills development with career progression*. Raising the level of qualifications of the workforce in order to raise the quality of the service and thus reduce inequalities amongst children and their families is central to the government's plan. There are critics who feel that many of these skills and knowledge are too prescriptive in the way they have to be demonstrated and we shall follow up some of these ideas later. Nevertheless, the EYFS and Common Core emphasise the need for consistency in children's experience, and high-quality practice in Early Years settings. The principles underpinning both documents are the same, originating from *Every Child Matters* with a focus on the well-being of the child and reflecting the five outcomes for children that you will be familiar with: be healthy, stay safe, enjoy and achieve in life, make a positive contribution, and achieve economic well-being. You can find more details of the six key areas of skills and knowledge at **www.everychildmatters.gov.uk/deliveringservices/commoncore/**.

Looking at these areas, you will see that the idea of teamwork and collaboration is embedded within each of them. They form a base for developing common values and standards of working amongst a team of practitioners across services and are relevant whether you are a member or leader of a team.

Working with other practitioners

Giving a collective name to those working in Early Years settings is not easy as they come from many different backgrounds and with a variety of qualifications. In this book they will be generally referred to as practitioners, occasionally as professionals and specifically, when applicable, as an Early Years Professional. Fumoto *et al* (2004, page 182) argue that the word *practitioner* is problematic because it *distracts our attention from taking a reflective view of teaching and learning*. We shall look later at some of the complexities of bringing together an Early Years service where there has been a historical division between education and care, which is still evident in the low status and pay for the majority of those who work there. The idea of a graduate-led profession has resulted in the introduction of the EYP, where teachers have previously been the only graduates in Early Years. The draft proposal for the newly formed lead professional in the Early Years (DfES, 2005b, page 36) put forward two possible titles for the role: *new teacher* or *social pedagogue*. There is much debate about these titles and particular connotations for the words teaching and pedagogy.

One argument is that the term *teacher* can put too much emphasis on the technical usage and does not necessarily imply the importance of the adult/child relationship in the learning (Fumoto *et al*, 2004). Siraj-Blatchford *et al* (2002) prefer the word *pedagogue*, which implies a balance between child-initiated and adult-initiated learning, and also reflective and reflexive practice on the part of the adult. The word *pedagogue* is widely used in Scandinavia, notably Denmark, but its meaning is closely linked with the training received there. Despite the intention to join up services, there is still a big division in Early Years between what settings are able to offer and the staff within them. Moss (2008, page 126) suggests that despite many obstacles – not least the way childcare is still regarded, with underpaid, untrained and undervalued practitioners – the UK should be looking to develop an Early Years service that offers *'education' in its broadest sense*. The discussions and debates are likely to continue about what an integrated Early Years service can offer. We shall return to this theme later.

REFLECTIVE TASK

1 *How would you describe yourself?*

2 *How do you see your role? Identify the following areas of responsibility within your role and say when you carry these out and with whom. You may not be carrying out all these responsibilities.*

  a *Leadership*

  b *Mentoring*

  c *Role-modelling*

  d *Supporting other colleagues*

  e *Being a member of a team*

3 *What particular skills, personal and professional, do you believe you bring to the job?*

Your role in a multiprofessional team

Standard 36 highlights the multiprofessional nature of your work. There will be further discussion on what being a *professional* means, but being able to collaborate with a range of practitioners is an essential part of your work. You, like many other practitioners, may always have developed working partnerships with other services. But these may have been dependent on an individual's commitment to sharing practice, or even have come about by chance. Multi-agency teams, a central notion of *Every Child Matters*, underpin the government's policy to improve the well-being of children and young people. You may work in a children's centre, seen as the heart of the government's programme because of their potential for providing a range of services from a 'hub' within the community. Some have been newly built or created from former buildings. But they can also be located in libraries, or a sports centre, village hall or health centre. The government's intention is to provide every community with a Sure Start children's centre, although these can vary in their structure.

The CWDC (2007a) identified three broad models of working across services. These models are not rigid, and looking at them in the box that follows you may well find you do not fit neatly into any of them, or you may find you work in some way within all three.

Multi-agency team

This is a group of practitioners seconded or recruited to a team with a common purpose and goals. Practitioners still maintain links with their home agency, receiving supervision and training from there. They may work together with individual children or sometimes with groups. The CWDC does not mention the higher-level teams that include local authorities and government. These are crucial in putting forward a coherent and cohesive strategic message for those working locally.

Multi-agency panel

Practitioners are employed by different agencies and meet regularly as a panel or network. They discuss children with additional needs who would benefit from multi-agency input. Individual practitioners carry out the work with children and families, although sometimes a key worker is employed to lead on case work. An example of this is the Behaviour and Education Support Team or an Early Years Intervention Team.

Integrated service

This is a 'visible service hub' in the community, with a range of services working in and from the same location, usually a Sure Start children's centre or extended school. There is a commitment from the partners to fund and facilitate integrated service delivery and a management structure that supports this.

(Adapted from: Early Years Foundation Stage: fact sheet on multi-agency working. You can find this at: **www.nationalstrategies.standards.dcsf.gov.uk/node/84355***.*

CASE STUDY

1 *Dee's title is Children's Centre Manager. Her immediate team comprises an administrator, outreach worker and peripatetic teacher. She sees her children's centre as the hub of the community with spokes going out that connect to other Early Years services. She describes the partnerships with others as virtual however, because there is no space for groups to meet in her building. She goes out to their settings.*

2 *Judy works at a nursery school and children's centre that is in the process of developing. It was originally a nursery school and now takes children from 6 months. It has not been possible to expand the original building but there has been some creative readapting to provide space for parents and community groups. There is a twice-weekly drop-in session for local parents instead of the original parent and toddler group. A health visitor and child psychologist come in on a sessional basis. The parent and toddler group is now a closed group for parents and babies. There is a class for parents with English as a second language, and crèche workers come in to assist with this.*

3 *Georgia is a childminder and since achieving EYPS has become a Foundation Stage Cluster Co-ordinator for Early Years. She works across private, voluntary and independent settings supporting practitioners and is involved in training. She also acts as a mentor for EYPS candidates.*

4 *Peggy manages a private part-time nursery and is one of the 'spokes' radiating from the 'hub', a Sure Start children's centre nearby. She feels the spoke is not yet well attached to the hub. She attends regular providers' meetings and is willing to give her support but feels that if she didn't attend these, she would miss out on information.*

REFLECTIVE TASK

- *How would you describe your setting?*

- *In what ways do you work multiprofessionally?*

- *How does it match up to the models described above?*

Working with individuals

The way you carry out your role and responsibilities will vary depending on where you work. But in common with everyone, you are part of a service that puts children and their families at the forefront of the service. A major part of your role as an EYP is to support others in developing a holistic approach to working with children and families. Whether the practitioners you work with, or you yourself, work mainly with the children or within the community, it is *what happens at the interface between service providers and service users that is critical* (DfES, 2007a, page 2).

The guidelines in *Effective practice: multi-agency working* conclude with the following:

Clearly, in order to build effective and trusting relationships we need to understand ourselves and to have the confidence to share more with others. This process of cultural change is essential if we are to provide better services to children and families.

(DfES, 2007a, page 6)

Understanding yourself, your strengths and weaknesses, is key to being able to support others in the team. In later chapters we look at the importance of developing emotional intelligence and at ways of communicating assertively with your colleagues. With all the changes in Early Years policy and practice, many practitioners, including you perhaps, are likely to have undergone some challenging and uncomfortable periods in their working lives. With demands for greater accountability from both the government and other professionals, some have lost their confidence, even if sometimes only temporarily.

To create an enabling environment where children love learning means practitioners need to have this love too (Anning and Edwards, 2006). You may have to challenge those who have been working in the same way for many years and find it hard to change. But your role as an EYP is to help other practitioners recognise and build on transferable skills, and identify relevant experience as they develop new roles and take on different responsibilities. Supporting adults in developing their learning bears many similarities to helping children learn, and we expand on this in a later chapter. Bringing to the fore what people might know already but not value, or indeed recognise, and doing this in such a way that they want to know more, is a crucial part of being an Early Years Professional.

C   H   A   P   T   E   R   S   U   M   M   A   R   Y

In this introductory chapter we have laid out the context in which you will be practising as a member of an Early Years team or teams, and asked you to think about your role and the setting in which you work. We have introduced some of the relevant government policy and raised some of the issues that will be followed up in the later chapters. These include the kind of team you work in; the range of roles, responsibilities and qualifications of others with whom you work; the problematic nature of giving a generic name to those who work in Early Years, and the different connotations of titles such as teacher or pedagogue, both considered as potential names for the role of the Early Years Professional. We end this chapter focusing on your role as an exemplar of good practice and a support to other members of your team.

Moving on

In the next chapter, we look at what teamwork involves and identify some of the characteristics of effective teams. You are asked to reflect on the teams you work in and your role as a member within them.

Self-assessment exercise

Please read each of the following statements and then answer the questions below for yourself. These questions relate to the issues that will be considered in the following chapters. You may want to return to this exercise after you have considered some of these.

Evaluation	Low–High				Comment
	1	2	3	4	
I have a clear understanding of my role and responsibilities in the particular setting I work in.					
I have a clear understanding of my role in a multi-agency service for children and families.					
I know when to take the lead and when to support as a team member.					
Others with whom I work have a clear understanding of their role and responsibilities.					
The team(s) I work with communicate well and members feel they are equal members.					
I find it easy to create a climate of confidence and trust amongst the staff I work with.					
I find it easy to consult others in my team and ask for suggestions.					
I take risks and make changes if I believe it will improve practice.					

FURTHER READING

Fumoto, H, Hargreaves, DJ, Maxwell S (2004) The concept of teaching: a reappraisal. *Early Years: An International Journal of Research and Development*, 24(2): 179–191.

2 The nature of teamwork

CHAPTER OBJECTIVES

This chapter introduces the concept of 'teamworking' in general terms and looks at some characteristics of effective teams. It outlines the various stages of development needed to create an effective team and some ways for assessing these. It considers the roles and responsibilities of team members and the contribution the EYP can make within a team. It gives you the opportunity to evaluate the groups you belong to and consider how you can enable collaboration and co-operativeness within them.

After reading this chapter, you should be able to:
- analyse the factors that differentiate a group from an effective team;
- examine your 'core' team and recognise the stage in its development;
- reflect on your role and responsibility within the team and what you can offer personally.

This chapter's main focus is on S33–S36 but it also refers to the standards for professional development, particularly S39.

Introduction

In its intention to create an *integrated workforce*, with *multi-disciplinary teams* (DfES, 2004, page 17), and *partnerships* across services (DfES, 2004, page 23), the government has raised the profile of teamwork in Early Years. You may work across services and be a member of several teams within or outside your setting. You could, for example, be a member of a team in the children's room, and be part of a senior management or specialist team. You may belong to a network of practitioners in your area who meet regularly, or even belong to a 'virtual' team, not meeting but communicating through information and communications technology (ICT). In this chapter, we ask you to focus mainly on what you would call your 'core' team that may or may not be multiprofessional. Later, we consider some of the challenges of working in the larger integrated workforce.

The Effective Provision of Preschool Education Project (Sylva *et al*, 2004) concluded that the qualifications of staff had a significant impact on the quality of practice and this, in turn, influenced the practice of the less qualified. The EYP guidance suggests that although EYPs carry out the same activities as their colleagues, they act as a role model by reflecting on their practice and need to be able to:

review, analyse and evaluate their own and others' practice and thus judge whether they are making a difference to the well-being, learning and development of children in their own and their colleagues' care.

(CWDC, 2008a, page 5)

Whether you take on the leadership in some contexts and act as a team member at other times, if, as Hay (2008, page 55) suggests, *the single biggest difference in children's emotional development could be achieved through peer support and teamwork*, then as an EYP, you have a major role to play within the team.

The history of teamwork

The democratisation of the workforce in the twentieth century with a less hierarchical management has changed the way we use language at work. There is a blurring of meaning, or confusion when commonly accepted words are used within different contexts (Hoag and Cooper, 2006). Teamwork is a common, if sometimes vague, concept in most working environments. There is much popular and academic literature – mainly on how to lead a successful team. Many job advertisements stress the importance of teamwork. There are management teams, virtual teams, production teams, sales teams and the word, team, often carries an implication that it is 'a good thing', almost a given. Waterstone's, the bookshop, for instance, suggests that their employees will be part of a *successful team*, Prêt à Manger advertises for *team members* for its sandwich bars. Job descriptions for Early Years practitioners usually mention the importance of being part of a team. We may label a group of people a 'team' but it takes more than a label to make them into one.

The word 'team' was first used in the ninth century to denote animals yoked together for ploughing; by the sixteenth century, its meaning had developed to describe people working together with a common goal. In the nineteenth century, its primary usage was in relation to sport, particularly cricket. The idea of 'teamwork' within work groups became a popular concept in the middle of the twentieth century, with the proliferation of literature on the nature of organisations. Its use in this context is therefore relatively new and its meaning needs to be used with care. So we begin by looking at how a disparate group of people can become a successful team.

A group or a team?

> ### REFLECTIVE TASK
>
> *Consider your work and social life and come up with some examples of when you were:*
>
> - *part of a group;*
>
> - *a member of a group;*
>
> - *part of a team;*
>
> - *a member of a team.*

Waiting for a bus, in a crowded café or at a party, we do not necessarily have any connection with or responsibility for others except for the place we find ourselves in or in the common pursuit. As a member of a group with a more focused interest, however, you are likely to have more in common; for example, you have children at the same school or attend an adult education class. There is a common goal, though again not necessarily a feeling of responsibility for others. Having a common goal is an essential element of any team, but to be effective requires more focus. All team members need an understanding of how they can contribute to achieve this common goal. They also need to feel a sense of belonging and experience good working relationships where people trust and value each other.

Rodd (2006, page 149) found that there was general agreement amongst Early Years practitioners on some common concepts for teams:

- the pursuit of a common philosophy, ideals and values;

- a commitment to working through the issues;

- shared responsibility;

- open and honest communication;

- access to a support system.

Indeed, practitioners deemed teamwork as positive; yet, from their past experience, in practice it appeared to be *quite a different proposition from teamwork in theory* (Rodd, 2006, page 150).

REFLECTIVE TASK

What is your experience currently, and in the past, of teamwork? Where do you think the challenges lie in moving teamwork from theory to practice?

Staff, although usually recruited through laid-down criteria, bring with them various personal and work histories. Practitioners' beliefs about and approach to education and childcare may not totally correspond to others'. We all have our own personal vision and base our views about the nature and significance of children's experiences in Early Years on the values we hold (David, 2007). The *Statutory Framework for The Early Years Foundation Stage* (DCSF, 2008b, page 7) stresses the importance of improving *quality and consistency* and developing a *universal set of standards*. Yet Moss and Pence (1994, page 173) suggest that: *quality childcare is, to a large extent, in the eye of the beholder* and it is true that there are many criteria by which to judge the quality. Unless practitioners come together to discuss and share views, we weaken our position as advocates for children, unable to articulate our views on what children need or to challenge policy and practice that does not place the child at the centre (Nutbrown, 2006).

In identifying the factors for successful multi-agency work, *Every Child Matters: change for children* stresses the need for a clear vision:

> *. . . to be translated into realistic goals, which reflect a grounded understanding of the needs of your target group and the support you have available to meet those needs. The goals should be revised in the light of experience.*
>
> *(www.everychildmatters.gov.uk?deliveringservices/multiagencyworking/successfactors/)*

Within any organisation, there will be a set of values that are both implicit and explicit. These underpin the setting's vision, and practitioners may either not understand them or, at worst, not even recognise them. Achieving a shared sense of purpose takes time and commitment as practitioners clarify how the underlying values affect the practice. Anning and Edwards (2006) cite Fullan's (1991) idea of a *false clarity* as often prevalent when the meaning of words is not fully explored. Practitioners accept certain practices, such as parental engagement as a 'good thing' but are not really clear about what this actually entails. Many settings offer a 'vision statement' that is given to parents or Ofsted. Who develops these will affect how they are translated and understood. We look at this further in Chapter 6.

Team members

Within your setting, it is likely that there will be a range of experience and qualifications as well as conditions of service. To be a strong team, it is important to have diversity amongst individuals, although this can be demanding when there are different attitudes or histories. Early Years practitioners frequently shy away from looking at differences amongst themselves. Working for long hours together, they value friendships and can therefore find it risky to review their work together critically. The *horizontal revolution* (Hoag and Cooper, 2006) that has brought a much flatter management structure in most organisations is evident in Early Years too. Practitioners work across disciplines and take on more responsibility. They are part of democratic teams that include children and parents and are asked to give their views, through their observations and records, and discuss issues with a range of professionals. This can be hard for some practitioners if they previously experienced a hierarchical management where they were not expected to take initiative and, indeed, were able if they wished to opt out of personal responsibility. Other practitioners may have been used to being the extroverts or 'stars', able to do things, without being accountable, in their own style; they can find it difficult to take a back seat in activities.

Teachers, for instance, who have been used to taking the lead with one or two nursery staff in a school situation, can find themselves in a flatter organisation such as a children's centre, where responsibilities are more widely spread. Other practitioners may regard teachers as opting out as their role changes as they become a much more integrated member of a team, with shared responsibilities. Childminders, too, as self-employed workers and with a tradition of working independently, may find it hard to feel part of an integrated team. They have often been regarded as a second choice to nurseries (National Childminders Association (NCMA), 2006) but as part of the overall structure are expected to work more closely with other services and may have a base in a children's centre. This can be a challenge for both sides as they come together. As described in an NCMA newsletter: *it is as if local authorities were asked to co-ordinate shopping opportunities, and privately-owned corner shops were asked to co-operate with Asda* (NCMA, 2006).

Much research has been done on successful personality types within work teams. There are inventories, commonly used, to analyse styles and personalities within a team, such as the Myers Briggs Type Inventory and the Thomas Kilman Conflict Style Inventory. Most notable is Belbin's Team Role Type Assessment, which is commonly referred to in the literature on teams. Belbin (1981), whose research was based on his practical work with teams of managers in training courses, identified a range of personality types within achieving teams. Members of a team only composed of creative and highly intelligent types, for example, did not necessarily get on with each other, nor get the task done. A team requires people with a variety of attributes. Below are brief descriptions of Belbin's team roles or types.

- *Co-ordinator – who presides over the group and keeps the group focused.*

- *Plant – who is creative and comes up with ideas and suggestions but is not interested in detail.*

- *Resource investigator – who is sociable and extrovert, liaising with others and bringing people together.*

- *Shaper – who likes to keep on task and brings people back when they go off track.*

- *Monitor evaluator – an analyser and dependable; looks at the detail.*

- *Teamworker – supportive to others and uncompetitive; popular but often in the background.*

- *Company worker – a good organiser and administrator.*

- *Finisher – good at meeting deadlines and checking details.*

You can download more information about these types at **www.belbin.com**

Looking at this range of personal attributes, you will notice that the team includes members who help to get tasks done, but also those who offer opportunities to explore new and creative ideas. Details do not get overlooked, and there is, most importantly, a co-ordinator who holds the team together.

Belbin carried out his research in a very particular context, and although his types certainly have relevance to Early Years' teams, they need to be used with caution. You can get stereotyped into a particular type. Having identified your favoured style or recognisable type, it is necessary to work on developing other skills and knowledge. In a small team of two or three people, say, it may be difficult to provide the same range of skills, knowledge and experience as a larger team, so it is important to acknowledge and value what each team member can contribute and build on this (Rodd, 2006). Talking to each other about how you work together and what you like or find difficult about each other's style is essential in developing teamwork. Early Years practitioners act as role models for children and speak on their behalf and have a responsibility for creating an environment that is:

fully inclusive of all children's needs, recognizing the need to respond to differences of ethnicity, culture, religion or belief, home language, family background, SEN, disability, gender or ability.

(DCSF, 2008a, page 41)

Yet actually discussing issues of equality and equity for children can be difficult for practitioners when it brings up differences in opinion. Whether you have an ethnically diverse team of practitioners or not, these issues need to be discussed if you are to offer a fully inclusive environment to children and their families.

PRACTICAL TASK

Consider the members of your team. Then reflect on the following:

1 Who am I most different from in personality or style of working?

In what ways? How does this affect our work together? Are there advantages and/or disadvantages in our differences? What do we need to do to work most effectively together?

2 Who am I most similar to? In what ways?

How does this affect our work together? Are there advantages and/or disadvantages in being similar in our approach and/or personality? What do we need to do to work most effectively together?

3. What are the strengths and weaknesses in the group which relate to differences and similarities in styles and personalities?

Please note: if you want to carry out this exercise with your team, be sure they have confidence in you and there is a reasonable level of trust amongst the team, or some practitioners may find it disturbing.

Doing this exercise at a training day, one practitioner felt able to say that the person she liked working with least was the one with whom she was most friendly. Their approach to children was very different. One was quiet, and especially skilful with individual children; the other was an extrovert and laughed and joked with the children. She felt her friend opted out by paying too much attention to individual children. In their discussion together afterwards, they were able to analyse their different styles and how these could complement each other.

Taking care of the team

Adair (1987) suggests that teams have three areas of need that have to be maintained and looked after:

- *the task* – this is the job; what has to be accomplished. The group will become frustrated if they do not achieve this;
- *the group* – the relationships between the workers need to be nurtured and maintained if the task is to be carried out;

- *the individual* – people's reasons for working vary. Being a member of a group may give people as much satisfaction as carrying out the task. Some individuals may want to take initiative; others may need more support.

Adair illustrates this idea by using three connecting circles to show how these needs have to be balanced. In Figure 2.1 below, you will see an adaptation of this to show how a team needs to develop each area. Too much focus on one either obliterates or imbalances the others.

Figure 2.1 Developing the needs of a team

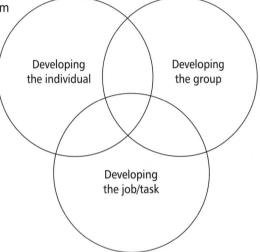

If for instance, you work together successfully in developing your practice with children with special needs, this will give the group a sense of achievement as well as a sense of satisfaction for the individual practitioners. If, however, one area of need is ignored for too long, difficulties may arise.

CASE STUDY

A new teacher joined a nursery class where the other practitioners had been for several years. She was highly qualified, energetic and full of new ideas and, after the initial meeting, the staff looked forward to her arrival. By half-term, the children's room was full of displays and the children's activities were well planned and of high quality. But things had gone badly wrong: one experienced nursery nurse went off sick; the other had lost her enthusiasm; the other less experienced teacher had lost confidence.

The case study above illustrates how the circles of need had become unbalanced; the teacher, in her eagerness, had concentrated on the task and had not attended to, or been aware of, the group's needs and had not encouraged the individuals to be fully involved and therefore motivated. This situation was later acknowledged when the group met together and, with an outside consultant, began to discuss and understand what had happened. There will obviously be times when it is important to focus mainly on the task, for instance when a new system is being introduced, but both the leader and team members need to be aware when it is time to refocus to maintain the other areas.

A developing team

Edgington (2004, page 54) highlights three types of team, common in Early Years. The *rigorous and challenging* team can at one level be successful in its capacity to analyse and make changes; the only danger is if it is never satisfied. Some teams find it hard to stop and celebrate their successes so that individuals feel satisfied with their work and valued for what they do. The *turbulent* team may on the surface appear to fulfil its aims and objectives, but the group itself is not cohesive and there is unresolved conflict. The *cosy* team gets on well together but is not able to look at itself critically, and avoids differences and challenges.

Teams are not static, however, and looking at how you are working and where your strengths and weakness lie is an ongoing process and part of the essence of being a team. You may have participated in one-off team-building training days but it is important to examine the team on a regular basis. Woodcock and Francis (1994) suggest that teams pass from an undeveloped to a mature stage as members become more trusting and clear of their roles and responsibilities. In the undeveloped team, the first stage, there is uncertainty; staff are not involved and not used to discussing issues or taking decisions. As they become more confident, they begin to 'experiment', discuss options, listen more carefully and take some risks. As the team 'consolidates', practitioners begin to establish ground rules and follow agreed procedures, accepting differences and recognising themselves as part of a group. The mature team has a high degree of flexibility, can prioritise and is able to experiment and discuss differences creatively. Like Adair's model, the task, group and individual needs are met. Mature teams are not easy to attain, nor indeed to maintain, and it is often the case that as team members increase in confidence and the team matures, individuals move on to take on further responsibility elsewhere – the nature of success.

CASE STUDY

Sally's team had worked together for 17 years and were – in her words – a 'cosy' team. They were content with what they were doing and parents liked what was on offer. Sally then had the opportunity to study for a foundation degree; she began to ask questions, see a link between the theory and practice, analyse the team's practice and make suggestions to extend the team's practice with the children. Her enthusiasm for what she was learning began to inspire the other team members. They wanted to know more and began to attend courses themselves. A very young practitioner, Donna, joined the team having completed a Diploma in Childcare and Education. Instead of disrupting the team, the others recognised her qualities and her skills, probably something they would not have done without experiencing Sally's enthusiasm. With Sally and Donna's input, the team is now working together on their planning, observation and assessment.

Tuckman's seminal work on team building (Tuckman, 1965; Tuckman and Jensen, 1977) is likely to be familiar to you. Like Woodcock and Francis (1994), he describes the evolutionary nature of teams. When a team begins 'forming' and coming together there is a period of getting to know each other and planning the way to work together. It is during this period that differences may begin to appear. Developing a forum where you trust each other means that practitioners become more honest. The next, 'storming', stage can be an uncomfortable period especially if there has not been a culture of openness before, or practitioners feel unease about speaking up in front of others with higher qualifications or more experience. There may be times when the group's or individual's views have to be challenged. For groups that have been working together for a while, old resentments may emerge. When engaging in discussions and reflecting on their work, team members need to feel confident that any difficulties will not be construed as weaknesses (Osterman and Kottkamp, 1993). As the team settles down (norming) and then begins to perform, it is important to continue the process of sharing experiences and reflecting on the work. Hay (2008, page 64) suggests Tuckman's model is like a ticking clock that represents the life cycle of the team and represents a way of looking at where the team is in its process; an adapted version of his model is shown in Figure 2.2.

To draw on Hay's analogy, it is likely that the clock needs winding up sometimes, or indeed stops. It may also need to be put back an hour or moved forward. Most teams go through stages where they lose energy and motivation, possibly because of changes, illness or other challenges. Change in the make-up of the team and in roles and responsibilities are inevitable, and these may slow down the process or, on the other hand, move the team forward.

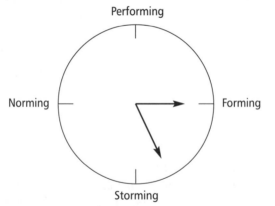

Figure 2.2 A team's progress
(adapted from Tuckman's model (1965))

The *Practice Guidance for the Early Years Foundation Stage* (DCSF, 2008c, page 8) stresses the adults' supportive role so children can:

• take risks and make mistakes;

• think creatively and imaginatively;

• communicate with others as they investigate and solve problems.

These are also key factors for effective teams but, ironically, some practitioners find it difficult or even dangerous to carry these out for themselves or in front of colleagues. If, however, they are to take on a supportive role for the children, they will need support from other adults as well. Hay (2008) suggests that the 'health' of the team depends very much on the relationships within it, whether people feel included, valued and able to contribute. The consequences of a 'healthy' team ensure that members then develop good relationships with children and families and can relate confidently to other agencies and groups within the community (Daly *et al*, 2004).

Working together

A series of radio programmes looked at the elements of teamwork in different contexts. The one below described a musical show. As you read about it, consider what is common to the teams you work with.

CASE STUDY

As well as dancers for this show, there are 65 backstage crew which include stage hands, musicians, dressers, sound and lighting, wardrobe and automation. Seven dressers with their own dressing plot help actors make the many changes; there are at least 500 costumes. There are many complicated cues for actors, lighting and stage managers but no-one panics, runs or bumps into each other. It is imperative that everyone works as a team for whether backstage or performing to the audience, they are all part of the action. Dr Tim Hopthrow (group psychologist from Kent University) analysed why this team worked:

- *common goal: this show was watched every day and had to keep up standards;*

- *size: there was an optimum size of team for the particular tasks;*

- *roles and responsibilities: people were clear about the task;*

- *co-ordination and collaboration: timing was essential for the three-hour show;*

- *language: the backstage crew used the same language as the actors – for instance the dressers worked on plots. This gave a sense that they were all in it together;*

- *trust: this had to be developed as dressers saw the actors naked or nearly naked;*

- *effective leadership and delegation: the director, when interviewed, said that she could not do everything and it was essential to trust people when she delegated.*

(BBC Radio 4, Team Spirit – first broadcast, 15 April 2008).

The components identified here are common to all successful teams. The members of the theatre team are interdependent but also working as individuals. They are all clear about the end product and united in putting on a good show. The backstage crew's contribution to the show is as essential as that of those who are on stage and receive the applause. In some Early Years settings, the 'backstage' crew's contribution gets overlooked. Staff, such as administrators or those who work in the kitchen do not always see themselves as key members of the team. Their insights about the setting and the children are valuable, coming from a different perspective (Rinaldi, 2006). They too need to be aware of their roles in fulfilling the five *Every Child Matters* outcomes. How clear are they in their responsibilities in, for example, helping children to *be healthy*, or *achieve economic well-being*?

You will notice the importance of having a common language; it is not coincidental that the backstage crew echo theatrical language, using the word *plots* for their spaces where they help actors to change. There is an ever-changing language in education that includes many acronyms and specialist words. Nothing takes away practitioners' confidence more than feeling that they do not understand what is being said. Nevertheless, some practitioners may need help to recognise that different professionals discuss issues in different ways, and as teams become more multiprofessional, they will also need to become more *multi-lingual* (Edwards, 2004, page 3). We shall look in later chapters at developing arenas where practitioners feel confident to ask questions and develop their practice through discussing it with others.

REFLECTIVE TASK

Think about the teams you are in. Are some members less 'visible' or even considered less 'valuable' than others? Consider the reasons for this. These may include their perceptions of team membership, how others see them or the way you meet together. Can you think of ways that would ensure that these people are included?

Sharing responsibility

Good leadership is key to a team's success, but successful leaders are dependent on their followers (Grint, 2005). As children's services become more inter-agency based, it is not possible to look to one leader who has all the answers; everyone working within it has a responsibility. In your role as an EYP, even if not a designated leader, there are opportunities to acquire and develop the skills and knowledge needed for leadership. Grint (2005) suggests that leadership is a craft that is learnt on the job, through reflective practice. He advocates setting up programmes where leaders can collaborate to look at real situations and learn as part of a team. Choosing the best player in the team to become captain does not make a sports team successful, he suggests. We need to look for *sustainable communities, not shooting stars* (Grint, 2005, page 2).

Having an opportunity to share responsibility was one of the common concepts that practitioners identified in Rodd's (2006) research on teamwork. Yet some responsibilities can be overlooked or considered less important than others. For instance, within certain parameters, key workers, parent liaison workers, the outings organiser, the head of kitchen, all have responsibilities. These will differ, some taking on more than others, but they all need to take the lead role at times. Rinaldi (2006), discussing the Reggio Emilia approach to early education – highly respected by many Early Years practitioners in the UK – emphasises the need for staff to communicate well with children, parents and colleagues and to create an environment where all feel able to share responsibilities. As part of the decision-making process, practitioners understand the importance of their contribution, but, as she suggests, they recognise *their inter-dependence on the quality of work of others* (Rinaldi, 2006, page 161). To be able to carry out their responsibilities, team members will need opportunities to discuss expectations and quality issues, to be kept up to date and consulted on new initiatives, and be involved in monitoring and evaluation. With a supportive and respectful team, practitioners are able to contribute with confidence, take initiative and develop personally and professionally. They can then take on fully their responsibility as a team member, which will involve, according to McCall and Lawler (2000, page 61), cited in Jones and Pound (2008):

- accepting a team culture which implies working honestly and fairly for the team, rather than for oneself;

- developing the capacity to work together and be prepared to learn as a team;

- working towards consensus decision making, as opposed to citing individual preference;

- being open-minded about tasks and obstacles, including facing change and trying out new ideas and methods;

- acting responsibly together, without the need for headteacher or 'lead manager' supervision;

- being willing to explain and justify the team's manner and modes of working, and modify these as necessary;

- accepting that teams, like individuals, are accountable for results.

PRACTICAL TASK

Look carefully at the list and highlight the ones that you think apply to your team at present.

Collaborating in your team

Earlier, I suggested that your experience and knowledge can be of great benefit to those who are less qualified. By recognising and understanding your own qualities and skills and being confident in what you offer means that you can assist and encourage others in recognising and valuing theirs. Goleman (1996) introduced the idea of emotional intelligence as a key quality for the workplace, suggesting that where emphasis on IQ leads to competitiveness, EQ (emotional intelligence quotient) leads to more co-operation. There has been much debate about what emotional intelligence actually constitutes, but Goleman has developed a model of competences: *personal competence* – the way we manage ourselves – and *social competence* – how we handle relationships. He argues that although managers within a commercial workplace may all have achieved an MBA, only some – those with a high degree of EQ – will be successful in the role. It is apparent that emotional intelligence is a prerequisite for developing relationships with others but, like IQ, the degree of EQ will be on a continuum. Teams are likely to be a good context to develop and increase EQ for, as Belbin's research suggests, the quality of interaction within a team, rather than the intellect, leads to success.

Nevertheless, emotional intelligence does not take the place of professional and technical abilities. You have to be competent at the job as well as self-aware and empathetic of others. Your competence and professionalism are prerequisites for influencing others in the way they practise and raising the quality of the setting (Moyles *et al*, 2002). 'Competence' and 'professionalism' however, need to be combined with emotional intelligence, or their meanings take on a static or distancing tone (Rinaldi, 2006). In looking at the way we collaborate with others, competence becomes *an approach, a willingness to work together*. It is *first and foremost an open process of professional development and self development, of mutual enrichment, and human willingness to work cooperatively and take joint responsibility* (Rinaldi, 2006, page 50).

Working towards EYPS gives you the opportunity to reflect on and develop your practice, to become a *mature and influential professional* (Pound, 2008, page 52). As the EYFS Principles into Practice (PiP) card 2.1 (DCSF, 2008d) suggests, your relationships with others in your team go hand-in-hand with effective practice with the children as you:

> *recognise the strengths of professional relationships in creating an approach that best meets the needs of individual children.*

As a senior or experienced member of the team, others will look to you for leadership and encouragement. At the same time, it is hoped you will derive support from the team. An understanding and sociable team, as Rodd (2006) suggests, helps you through some of the inevitable stresses and tensions that arise when working in Early Years. Much job satisfaction comes from being a member of a supportive team, and a good team can nurture you professionally and personally.

C H A P T E R   S U M M A R Y

In this chapter, we have looked, in general terms, at the nature of teams, the role and responsibilities of the members and your role within the team. We have considered teamwork as a process based on democratic practice, dialogue and shared understandings. You have reflected on your 'core' team and its stage of development and considered some ways of translating the theory of teamwork into practice.

Moving on

In the next chapter, we consider how the larger organisational framework affects the way teams function and how the structure impacts on your work. We consider some definitions of leadership and how different styles of leadership affect teamwork and look at how the unique cultures of organisations affect collaboration.

Self-assessment exercise

Remembering that teams develop and move through stages, choose one team that you are a member of or lead. Look at some elements of teamwork listed below, then score each one from 5 to 1 according to how you think your team works (5 = highest, very well; 1 = lowest, not so good). Comment on the evidence you have for your scoring and the action you conclude is needed to improve as a team. Look at what your role could be in supporting this action.

When you have done this, look back at Woodcock and Francis' (1994) and Tuckman's (Tuckman, 1965; Tuckman and Jensen, 1977) descriptions of team development and see what stage you think your team is at.

	Score	Comment	Action needed	My role
Trust Has the team established ground rules?				
Empathy Can the team see other viewpoints including those of the children, their families and other practitioners?				
Active Do all members take an active part in the team?				
Monitor Does the team look regularly at how members are working together?				
Work together Does the team collaborate?				
Open to opportunities How far is the team ready to try out new ideas and take risks?				
Responsible Are individual members prepared to accept responsibility and not always rely on the leader?				
Knowledge Are members of the team confident about contributing ideas and asking questions?				
The stage the team is at on <date> is:				

Rodd, J (2006) Building and leading a team, Chapter 8, in: *Leadership in early childhood*, 3rd edition. Maidenhead: Open University Press.

3 Looking at your organisation

CHAPTER OBJECTIVES

This chapter considers the framework within which teams function. It draws attention to the key features of an organisation, which can be both formal and informal in nature, and how these affect a team's development and success. It looks at some definitions of leadership, with particular focus on those that are applicable to leading a team. It suggests that the EYP needs to be aware of the culture of organisations and how this may affect the communication and integration of a team.

After reading this chapter, you should be able to:
- summarise the key features of an organisation;
- discuss appropriate styles of leadership for leading a team;
- reflect on your own organisation and how the culture affects the practice.

This chapter focuses particularly on Standards 33 and 35, with reference to the framework within which teamwork and collaboration can flourish. It also links to S4 and S6 suggesting that the framework will also have implications for what your setting offers to children.

Introduction

Handy (1993, page 20) suggests that the theory of *organising started out simple but got steadily more complicated*. It is not the remit of this book to look in detail at all the theories and schools of thought about organisations but to draw your attention to some of the factors of the organisation that may inhibit or enhance the way you work as a team. An organisation can mean the setting or institution itself. But it also refers to the way things are 'organised' and put into practice. Settings need a framework so that decisions get made, practice develops, and people can go about their work, feeling motivated and with clear goals. Without organisation, there is conflict and confusion. Since much of the work of Early Years practitioners focuses on people – children and adults – and their relationships, there is a tendency to blame them when things go wrong: the parent couldn't cope; *x* and *y* cannot work together. People are certainly a major component in organisations but there are other elements that may help or hinder the way you work together. Becoming aware of how these affect your practice and relationships helps you to make some concrete changes and learn to manage aspects of the work that cannot be changed easily or may take time to establish.

Creating a new organisation

A former day nursery was converted into a children's centre with a Sure Start team who moved into their building. Before this took place the day nursery had had to split into two groups and move into temporary accommodation while the building work took place. They moved back into a much-improved building. However, the way the space was arranged had implications for the way the teams would come together. The Sure Start team's office and meeting rooms were separated from the main part of the nursery by the entrance hall. The new manager for the Sure Start team and the existing manager of the day nursery each had their own offices. They were both finding their jobs strenuous but tried to meet formally weekly and to see each other informally each day. Many of the Sure Start team, now based at the centre but already familiar with the local community, were out much of the day; the day nursery staff worked shifts. The day nursery staff were asked to give parents information about the other services but knew little about them. Parent groups took place in a room far from the children's rooms and although some parents used both services, there appeared to be no connection between the two.

It was obvious that this new service was not going to run smoothly; the structure, systems, people and culture all needed to be looked at.

1 *The structure*: this refers to the size, the function, the space and the management structure. These had all changed with the coming together of the two teams. The way the rooms were organised worked against easy integration. Staff in the Sure Start team worked fairly autonomously, with a specific role in the community, and belonged to other teams such as health and social services; they expected to discuss and give their opinion on issues that were happening. The day nursery staff worked in a much more hierarchical structure with a senior management team.

2 *The systems*: there was an obvious need to consider the communication systems between the managers and between the two teams. There were separate systems for accountability. The financial ones posed potential conflict as the service expanded and decisions had to be made about priorities.

3 *The people*: the staff were unclear about each other's roles and responsibilities. Although the two managers endeavoured to work together, they were not involved with each other's teams. The nursery staff had had a year in temporary accommodation and needed opportunities to come together again as one team. The Sure Start team and the nursery team did not see themselves as an integrated or interprofessional team despite the fact that the organisation now had a common name: a children's centre.

4 *The culture*: this refers to the history of the organisation and the behaviour and expectations of the people within it. The two teams brought with them separate histories of working and different attitudes to work. Their behaviour together and the perception of their roles differed tremendously.

REFLECTIVE TASK

Consider the four elements of organisations described above: structure, systems, people, culture, and look again at the case study. Taking into account some of the criteria for effective teams that you looked at in the last chapter, reflect on:

- *the actions you would take as an EYP, either as a member of the day nursery team or the Sure Start team, to help improve the understanding and communication between the two teams. These could be formal or informal actions.*

What kind of organisation?

The word organisation is related to *organism*, something that is living and therefore changing. Any organisation that is dynamic will, like any organism, live and grow, and its shape and boundaries are likely to change. You may find it difficult to see your place within a precise organisation. Does the organisation you belong to feel defined or is it flexible? Are the boundaries blurred? Are you part of several organisations, within a large universal service for children and their families, or a member of a much smaller organisation providing a particular service but linking with others? Within an organisation there will be different levels or subsets (Coleman, 2005), so although you may see yourself as part of a large organisation you are also likely to work within one of the subsets. Organisations may vary in their size and purpose but, whether formal or informal, have some common features.

CASE STUDY

Carol set up a parent and toddler group a few years ago in a community hall. It was very informal and proved popular with local parents. She wanted to make sure it was inclusive and she visited families in the community to tell them about it. When advertising it in the neighbourhood, she explained what its purpose was and the importance of welcoming anyone with a toddler. As it grew, she found that she had to set down certain boundaries about time, helping out and the parents' role and responsibilities within the group.

On the surface, Carol's group was very relaxed and parents and carers developed good friendships with each other. But it was more than a social group and had most of the basic features of an organisation that works well. It existed for a definite purpose and developed:

- defined goals;

- an identifiable membership group;

- clear boundaries;

- people collaborating together;

- a formal structure – its various tasks were clearly defined and grouped together into jobs;

- activities that were formally co-ordinated. Rules and procedures existed so that people performing the organisation's tasks could achieve its purpose.

(adapted from Gallagher *et al*, 1997, page 224)

REFLECTIVE TASK

Look at the features above and, reflecting on the nature of the setting you work in, see if you can identify these features within it.

CASE STUDY *continued*

Carol was very clear about the reason for the parent and toddler group's existence. It was a safe place for children to experience play activities. Parents could spend time with their children in friendly surroundings and also get advice and information from the other adults. She knew that some parents would have no difficulty in coming to the group but realised it was particularly important to reach those parents who were isolated, did not speak English as a first language or who might find it difficult to join a group. The group's informality was a key factor in its success, as parents felt very welcome and unpressurised, but within this informality there had to be certain boundaries. As the group grew, many of the boundaries developed through discussion with parents. Some of these seemed minor, such as where to leave buggies (these could become a safety hazard if not put away in the right place) or closing time (the centre had to be cleared and cleaned for other users). Others concerned expectations around behaviour amongst adults and children. Carol and her staff supported the parents involved when, for example, a toddler hit another one but parents were ultimately responsible for their children. New issues arose as the group developed, such as a parent bringing in a schoolchild who, not well, was off school. In the short term, an informal discussion with the parent resolved this and she went home. But in the longer term, a more formal rule had to be introduced so that people were clear. Carol saw herself as the main facilitator and accountable to her funders, but she encouraged parents to take a more active part in decision making. She introduced meetings to discuss ideas and encouraged them to give feedback. The group remained informal but the structure developed and became clearer.

A reason to exist

A major factor for an organisation's success is that members understand and are clear about its reason for existence and purpose. This may seem an obvious point but it is surprising how many practitioners are not clear because this is not explicitly discussed. The primary reason for your 'organisation's' existence is unlikely to have altered much despite undergoing external policy changes. The children are still the main reason for your work. But the introduction of a universal service for children and families with the five defined outcomes of *Every Child Matters* has made the reason for your existence more explicit. Some practitioners whose main role continues to be working directly with the children may not be fully aware of their contribution to a universal service. As you observed in the day nursery and Sure Start team case study at the beginning of this chapter, it was vital for staff to meet together to understand that, although their responsibilities were different, they all had a common reason to exist. Genuine collaboration will only take place when practitioners understand their role in helping to fulfil these outcomes for children within a larger context. If there are no clearly defined goals, then conflict may arise as practitioners work at cross-purposes.

PRACTICAL TASK

In one sentence, sum up the reason for your setting's existence.

What sort of structure?

A structure sets out who does what, how jobs and activities are carried out, who reports to whom and who has authority. Structures can be hierarchical and also flexible, but to support successful teamwork they need to be clear and transparent. This applies to a small team such as a pre-school playgroup where members may have to take on several responsibilities. How you group the children, who is their key person, how shifts are organised support the effectiveness of what you offer to children and families. With a range of practitioners in loose teams, there can be confusion about the structure, such as who takes responsibility and who manages. Children's centres often have a large staff, working different shifts and with a variety of roles. Managing these is a complex task and usually leads to a hierarchical structure and defined roles. Siraj-Blatchford *et al* (2007) suggest this can be very effective, and could be the most efficient way of organising but that there is a danger if it diminishes the opportunities for teamwork and decision making. The concept of *democratic professionalism* (Oberheumer, 2005) exemplifies a model of *distributive leadership*. There may be a hierarchical management structure, but the leaders delegate tasks and appreciate and maximise specialist knowledge. This kind of leadership creates a participatory culture where groups share their knowledge and evaluate together.

Who leads?

Siraj-Blatchford and Manni (2006) suggest that it may seem paradoxical that it is strong leadership that allows collaboration and teamwork. Defining leadership in the Early Years sector is complex, as services join up and practitioners find themselves leading one or several teams with a range of professionals. Not having a common name for the leader in Early Years can also be confusing (Moyles, 2006); you may be in a setting with a 'manager', a 'head', 'leader' or ' supervisor', or as a childminder linked to an 'adviser'. In their *Effective Leadership in the Early Years Sector (ELEYS) Study*, Siraj-Blatchford and Manni (2006) looked at a range of leadership theories, and drawing on previously cited effective settings (Siraj-Blatchford *et al*, 2002, 2003), posed the question: *what is effective educational leadership in the early years?* They examined definitions for leadership and identified that *contextual literacy*, *collaboration* and the *improvement of children's learning outcomes* as the fundamental requirements found in effective settings (Siraj-Blatchford and Manni, 2006, page 26). They cite Southworth's (1998) notion of *situational leadership*, where the leader develops *contextual literacy* and thus is able to *read* the situation as well as take account of the people in it. This is particularly relevant for multiprofessional teams where a diverse group of people may work together in newly created contexts. Contextual literacy requires an understanding of settings as *dynamic organisms* (Siraj-Blatchford and Manni, 2006, page 14). As circumstances shift with changes of practitioners or families or the introduction of new policies and practice, the team will have to adjust to *make room for new energies, ideas and conflicts* (ibid, page 14). You looked in Chapter 2 at the need for leaders to have followers. Moyles *et al* (2002, page 130) argue that effective pedagogical practices depend on leaders who develop *a strong overall management and organisation ethos in which practitioners feel they are important, valued and have status*. Siraj-Blatchford's and Manni's study (2006, page 26) underlined the importance of leaders who could engender the kind of collaboration where practitioners can discuss and share different ideas and where a learning culture allows people to examine their own practice confidently.

CASE STUDY

Judy has taken on the role of community services leader in a children's centre, having been the deputy of the nursery previously. She has mainly part-time staff in her immediate team and also meets with the local health visitors, social worker, and educational psychologist and on occasions with people from arts organisations.

I'm doing a job I've never done before and nor has anyone else in some of the things we do. I am not expert like I felt when I managed in the nursery. I'm having to learn about different models of working and managing people who have had completely different experience from me. Some of them, such as the outreach workers, are also new to the job. The political position is different when you work from outside in. Staff in the nursery don't always recognise what we are offering, and complain that parents coming in to use the facilities in the centre sometimes disrupt their sessions. It's interesting and engaging and working with others is expanding my horizons. But it's taking time to feel comfortable.

> **REFLECTIVE TASK**
>
> *Having read about Judy's new appointment leading a team, and bearing in mind Southworth's (1998) notion of contextual literacy, what practical action do you think Judy could take to:*
>
> - *help the staff she works with become confident in their roles?*
>
> - *remain confident in her own leadership abilities as she takes on a very different role from her previous one?*
>
> - *help her core team to feel part of the larger 'organisation'?*

Styles of leadership

Many Early Years researchers have identified and categorised particular styles of leadership. Rodd (2006, page 39) cites Neugebauer's (1985), four major styles of leadership that are manifest within Early Years settings:

- the taskmaster;

- the comrade;

- the motivator;

- the unleader.

When discussing styles of leadership, it is important to see them on a continuum. The authoritarian (taskmaster) puts little emphasis on developing relationships and focuses on getting the task done; at the other extreme is the laissez-faire leader (the unleader) who leaves things to chance and allows people to get on in their own way. The comrade puts a good deal of emphasis on relationships but little on task. The motivator style combines an attention to relationships and a concentration on high-quality practice, generally seen as the most appropriate leadership style in Early Years (Rodd, 2006, page 40). One particular style might not suit every context however. Siraj-Blatchford and Manni (2006) suggest that *distributed* leadership, found in effective settings where practitioners collaborate as a team and where leaders delegate, is not possible unless staff are experienced enough to take on specialist tasks and responsibilities. The leader may have to be much more directive and focus on the process of developing a team that feels confident and skilled before this happens. There may be a place for a taskmaster, where quality is poor and staff are not carrying out their responsibilities. Likewise, the comrade style could be appropriate where there is low morale within the setting, where individuals need extra support or team relationships need to be developed. You will remember in Chapter 2 you looked at the importance of keeping in mind the individual, group and task needs if a team is to develop successfully.

1 Hayley was appointed manager of a new purpose-built private nursery in a corporate chain. There was plenty of space and all new furniture and equipment. She was a very experienced practitioner, having been an adviser in social services and run a large local authority day nursery. She found, however, that half the staff, although holding Early Years qualifications, had had little experience and, in some cases, had little commitment to the job. Her concern was to create an environment where parents and children were respected and where staff felt confident and responsible. She found it difficult to delegate or take time off because both staff and parents relied on her for advice and information. Although not naturally 'a taskmaster', she found this the most appropriate style with certain members of staff as she demanded higher standards of practice. There was no possibility, at this stage, of building a cohesive team when individuals were not sharing the same values and beliefs about working with children.

2 Briony followed a leader with a predominantly 'comrade' style. Relationships were friendly and supportive amongst staff and with families. But she felt that staff were not making the most of the opportunities for developing children's learning. She found them easy to work with and gradually introduced ways for staff to listen to and observe children and reflect on their practice, bringing in outside specialists to help them evaluate children's play. Briony modelled the practice she wanted to see with the children. Her motivator style did not suit everyone, particularly some of the more senior staff, who found it hard to take on the additional responsibility she expected, having previously been able to exist with an 'unleader' style. However, over a couple of years, Briony's team members were beginning to discuss their practice reflectively and the quality of interaction with the children had increased considerably.

Taking into account Neugebauer's four styles of leadership, look at the following examples and consider your role and responsibilities in the following scenarios. As an EYP, how would you respond to the situations and what areas would you concentrate on to help develop a cohesive and effective team, whether as a member or leader of the team?

1 You have replaced a member of staff who was well organised and much liked. The team is functioning well and the staff often refer to her and how well she worked with them.

2 There is a continuous turnover of staff and many agency staff. Some staff are feeling unsettled.

3 There is a serious rift amongst staff that is affecting the way people are working together. The work with the children is suffering.

4 You want to make a radical change in practice and it is likely some staff will find this difficult.

5 *The team is not used to taking decisions and waits for you to make suggestions and take the lead. You would like them to develop and take on more responsibility.*

6 *Your line manager, who you like as a person, has a different leadership style from yours.*

Number	My response to the situation	Priorities/strategies to develop a cohesive and effective team
1		
2		
3		
4		
5		
6		

Systems

We suggested earlier in the chapter that 'organisation' also refers to the way things are done or carried out. With the current need for paperwork to demonstrate accountability, 'systems' have acquired a bad reputation in some quarters. But Handy (1988, page 121), in his analogy of an organisation as a body, sees the structure as the skeleton and the systems as the 'nerves'. The nervous system alerts the body and allows you to plan ahead and recognise when something is not right, helping to keep the body healthy.

A practitioner who was promoted to children's centre manager expressed her concern when told it would be a much more 'strategic' role. Having worked with the children for many years whilst taking on increasing responsibility, she was worried that 'strategic' implied losing touch with them.

> *I realised she said that was not what 'strategic' was about. It was actually taking a wider view, looking at resources, health and safety, monitoring quality and*

making sure the systems we had were in place and operational. I like it now, because in my position I can make things happen for the benefit of the children. I still have lots of contact with children and parents and the staff. But we have to be accountable. Working with other services, we have to know how things work here so we can work with them.

Many of your systems may happen informally but as services become increasingly integrated, monitoring systems are becoming more complex. They should be there to support not to restrict, and as Hay (2008, page 75) points out, systems are sometimes disrupted and are often not perfect but *need to work for people most of the time*. The major reason that the day nursery and Sure Start children's centre, described earlier, began to improve was because systems were put into place that supported children and families and the staff. Practitioners usually blame 'communication' when things go wrong. Apart from personal communication, the systems by which you give and receive information need to be reviewed regularly. We look further at this in Chapter 8 when we consider the broad context of multi-agency work and the increasing reliance on information technology. Within your immediate team there will be the formal systems such as plans and records, and monitoring and evaluation meetings, and also the informal ones such as day-to-day discussions and written aide-mémoires like the staff notice board. On an individual level, if you meet regularly, much of the information sharing can happen informally, as you plan together in the office or staff room. But Anning *et al* (2006) highlight the danger of excluding part-timers and suggest that physical space too impacts on the way practitioners share information. For example, peripatetic staff and those who do not have a specified space in the building, and come in infrequently, can miss out on information. Depending on one particular method is not likely to work either. Communication systems need backup as people are bombarded with more and more information, only some of which is relevant to them. Reminding your colleagues may seem irritating, but is essential until a system is really embedded.

Systems for accountability are not always clear. Some of you will be in a setting with a management or governing body, others will be accountable to the owner. Your management system should provide practitioners with a clear understanding of their role and responsibilities about who makes decisions, how procedures are carried out, and what are the priorities. Practitioners working as key workers with individual children need to understand the systems for gathering knowledge and feeding this back to the team. Key workers usually establish relationships with the parents and will need to be aware of who else is working with the family and their role within this.

The *Every Child Matters'* toolkit for working in multi-agency teams suggests that in order to work to common goals, it is important to develop the same procedures around the following policies:

- safeguarding and promoting the welfare of children, including child protection;
- diversity and equal opportunities;

- home visits;

- identity checks;

- ethical framework;

- compliments, complaints and grievances;

- disciplinary procedure.

(**www.everychildmatters.gov.uk/deliveringservices/
multiagencyworking/managerstoolkit/systemsandprocesses/**)

This may mean adopting a policy from another agency or adapting one of yours. It may involve creating a new joint policy. Looking at your systems and reviewing the policies as a team is a good starting point for exploring the differing views practitioners may have on how to put these into practice and a way of discussing the underlying values and cultural norms.

REFLECTIVE TASK

- *Look at the list of policies above.*

- *Begin with the policy for safeguarding and promoting children's welfare including child protection. Reflect on your understanding of the procedures for this in your setting and decide how clear you are about them. Then consider if there is agreement in your team about how these procedures are carried out.*

- *Choose three other polices from above and one other policy particular to your setting and go through the same process as described above.*

Procedures for:	Am I clear? Yes/partially/no	Is the team in agreement? Yes/no	Action I need to take
1 Safeguarding and promoting the welfare of children, including child protection			
2			
3			
4			
5 (Policy from your setting)			

Culture of an organisation

Much has been written about organisational cultures, and this chapter can only touch on some of its complexities. The culture of an organisation pervades what and how you do things. An influential writer on organisations, Schein (1992) argues that culture develops through shared experiences as an organisation tries to achieve consistency and become an integrated body. Members of the organisation develop a collective pool of knowledge and new members take on accepted norms of behaviour. Individuals, especially those in leadership positions, shape the culture positively or negatively. Developing a consistency and shared understandings can obviously be a positive but there is a danger when assumptions are not questioned. Healthy cultures are fluid and continuously shifting and changing shape (Morgan, 1997; Schein, 1992).

As it is not easy to identify, Handy (1993, page 191) suggests you *perceive* or *feel* the culture of an organisation and you recognise it in the particular way people behave, their attitudes and beliefs. It is when you come up against difficulties in changing certain aspects in your setting that you may well recognise its power. The *Every Child Matters* advice (**www.everychildmatters.gov.uk/deliveringservices/multiagencyworking/manager stoolkit/managingchange/organisationalculture/**) compares organisational culture to a tree, with beliefs at the roots, the norms forming the trunk, values as a branch and behaviour as the leaves (Figure 3.1).

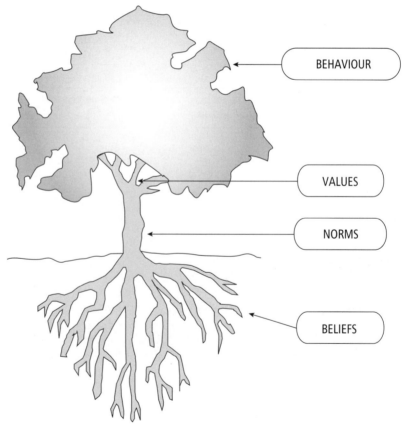

BEHAVIOUR

VALUES

NORMS

BELIEFS

Figure 3.1
Organisational
culture

How people behave in the organisation will depend on their understanding of the team's or setting's norms and their personal or professional values and underlying beliefs. These can go deep. The culture within Early Years settings not only affects the way practitioners work together but, even more crucially, what they offer the children and their families. For example, a belief that childcare does not involve teaching and learning can affect the way practitioners and others behave towards each other. Practitioners who are confident that those who work in Early Years are as valuable as those in school or within other services will fight to be recognised. But not all feel able to do this. Moss (2008, page 123) argues that it is only when it is accepted that a more qualified workforce rests in the belief that early years has status – and is not just a job that all women do, 'unpaid and untrained, in the home' – that the culture will change. With the very small percentage of men who work – just over 2 per cent according to the Daycare Trust and TUC (2008, page 7) – this idea that caring for children is a woman's job is reinforced. Although research carried out showed that parents wanted more male workers in Early Years, particularly lone parents, there is still a difficulty of overcoming some of the stereotypes.

CASE STUDY

Scott has noticed the difference since his setting became a children's centre. There are more male workers coming into the centre although he is still the only man working directly with children:

> *When I first arrived, I was made to feel 'special' both in a good and bad way. I was the token man and so people expected me to respond in that way. It's like asking someone from Bangladesh to speak for the whole population. In fact, I'm not very interested in football and hopeless at DIY. Gradually parents and staff began to see the real me. I hate that thing women say 'all men are the same'. It's going to take a long time to get rid of the negative feelings about men working with young children. Lots of places are working hard to encourage fathers to come in with their children, but this is still a 'special' occasion. There's years of prejudice to get over. It's only when there are plenty of us around that the culture will change.*

REFLECTIVE TASK

- *Do you recognise any barriers against the employment of men in Early Years and do you think these are prevalent in your setting?*

- *If you have men working in your setting, what roles and responsibilities do they take on? How do you think the presence of men in an Early Years setting changes the culture?*

Aubrey *et al* (2000) argue that the impact of the cultural context and beliefs shapes the approach that adults take towards their understanding of childhood and children's potential. For example, the *Every Child Matters* agenda emphasises the role of the practitioner in allowing even very young children to be an integral part of decision making, and a current concern for many researchers and practitioners is how we really listen to children. This can mean a cultural shift amongst practitioners as they move from being the powerful 'givers' to being on the receiving end of children's perspectives and views.

Each organisation creates its own unique culture and this will influence how it changes and develops. The culture may emanate from the top and be based on the leader's values; it may have developed almost unconsciously through practitioners' actions and beliefs; it may or may not be a shared culture or there may be several cultures within an organisation. Both Briony and Hayley, whom you read about earlier, were involved in trying to shift the culture. Cultures grow and shift but are very powerful. They manifest themselves through the way people use language with children and adults, their attitudes towards the children and even the objects and pictures displayed. New attitudes and beliefs have to be embedded if they are to affect the practice.

CASE STUDY

A group of practitioners at a playgroup are struggling with putting the EYFS into place. One described the difficulty:

> *. . . we know we are supposed to be child-centred in our work and we talk about this but we still find it hard to do this as it takes so long to finish our displays or make cards and presents for the parents. It seems we are doing it half and half now.*

Values and norms may be stated or implicit. This comes out through the group's behaviour. For example, there may be in-jokes, not understood by anyone who comes new to the group, or ways of relating to children or parents that are not openly discussed. On the other hand, there may be an explicit culture founded on principles such as those in the EYFS, where each child is seen as unique and an enabling environment nurtures positive relationships and opportunities for learning and development. This will have come as a result of practitioners, children and parents talking, understanding the vision and purpose and actively pursuing this together.

A key challenge for multiprofessional working is understanding the different cultures from which practitioners have come. As services join together and practitioners work more closely as integrated teams, the different individual organisational cultures may surface. Practitioners with similar backgrounds may take for granted particular ways of doing things or certain ideas as a given. This can be uncomfortable for those joining them, or those who do not fit in with the prevailing attitudes, whether children and families or practitioners. Practitioners need to be aware of assumptions they may make about others, or about children and families or how the use of language or ways of communicating can exclude. They may have to re-examine and perhaps change individual practice, leaving their former professional comfort zone as they look at issues in new ways (Jones, 2008). How these changes are managed, McCullogh (2007) suggests, could be *predictive* of how successful integrated services become.

> ### REFLECTIVE TASK
>
> *This is not an easy task and you may like to discuss this with other practitioners. Consider your setting and, referring to the tree diagram (Figure 3.1), try to identify some of the following in your team. Consider whether they are implicit or explicit:*
>
> - *beliefs;*
>
> - *norms;*
>
> - *values.*
>
> *Say what you perceive or feel that makes you come to this conclusion and how they manifest themselves in your team's behaviour.*

Handy (1993) lists some of the factors that influence the organisational culture. As you read them, consider how these might influence what happens in your setting.

History and ownership

You may be working for a chain of private nurseries where there is a corporate image; you dress uniformly or the equipment is bought centrally. There may be one owner who either works on-site or appears occasionally, or you may have a management committee or a governing body. The way these operate will influence the way your setting is organised. The history too will affect those within the setting as well as those without. Are you a new setting or a transformed one and does the setting have a particular reputation? What does the name imply? One nursery school that developed a children's centre with an integrated team nevertheless decided to keep 'nursery school and children's centre' in its name because it was long established and well-known in the neighbourhood. In fact, few people referred to it by either of these but just by its name, denoting how established it was.

Size

Inevitably, larger organisations have to be more formalised with subsets and formal systems of communication. Size is likely to affect the way the organisation is managed and there may have to be more formalised systems of communication.

Like Dee in Chapter 1 you may work with a very small immediate team but have a large number of contacts. A large organisation does not mean that it is not friendly; it could, in fact, be easier to develop good relationships with colleagues where there is a variety of people.

Goals and objectives

The goals and objectives will change over time but there may also be those that are never discussed. Hayley, working in a private nursery, noted a hidden agenda, which was never openly discussed, about children's attendance. To break even, the nursery needed a certain number of children to attend. Briony was aware that although the goals and objectives were written in a statement, these were not followed through.

The environment

How your setting works will be influenced by where it is and who is in it. Compare a playgroup which rents the church hall and has little space for the children to play outside with a purpose-built children's centre. Both may be offering high-quality practice but in very different circumstances. Who is in that environment and the ethos they have created will affect what goes on within it.

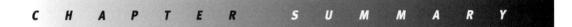

CHAPTER SUMMARY

This chapter has looked at the importance of the framework for teamwork to develop successfully. It has stressed the importance of practitioners understanding the different factors of an organisation that will affect the way they work together, such as the structure, the systems, the leadership and the culture. It has asked you to reflect on these in relation to your own workplace and to consider what you as an EYP can do to clarify these so that your team becomes more cohesive and effective.

Moving on

The next chapter discusses the need for teams that communicate assertively and your role as an individual in encouraging this. It looks at the different types of behaviour that can inhibit or help the way you exchange information with your colleagues, giving examples of passive and aggressive behaviour and distinguishing this from assertiveness. It suggests ways for putting over your point of view clearly, setting boundaries when appropriate and understanding why some situations are more difficult to manage than others.

FURTHER READING

Hofkins, D (2008). Men at work. *The Guardian*, 22 January 2008. **www.guardian.co.uk/education/ 2008/jan/22/schools.earlyyearseducation** (accessed 27 March 2009).

Siraj-Blatchford, I, Manni, L (2006) *Effective leadership in the early years sector: the ELEYS study.* London: Institute of Education, University of London.

www.gtce.org.uk/shared/contentlibs/126795/93128/120213/eleys_study.pdf (accessed 27 March 2009).

Whalley, ME (2008) Leadership in the Early Years: a review of the literature, Chapter 2, in: *Leading practice in Early Years settings.* Exeter: Learning Matters.

USEFUL WEBSITES

Every child matters: change for children: *multi-agency services: toolkit for managers.*
www.everychildmatters.gov.uk/deliveringservices/multiagencyworking/managerstoolkit/
(accessed 27 March 2009).

4 Communicating assertively with your team

CHAPTER OBJECTIVES

This chapter focuses on your responsibility to raise issues and put forward your ideas within the team, and highlights some of the essential skills for communicating assertively. It asks you to consider the reasons why you may find it more difficult to communicate assertively in some situations than others. It looks at how your feelings affect your behaviour and how this, in turn, can influence others' responses positively or negatively. It introduces you to some skills for making requests, putting your point over and setting boundaries by saying 'no'. Later chapters will look at assertive ways to handle criticism and give 'critical' feedback to others.

After reading this chapter, you should be able to:
*   understand what being assertive means and how this differs from aggression;
*   recognise some of the feelings that stop you and other practitioners from communicating clearly and directly;
*   examine some strategies for communicating more assertively in difficult situations.

With its focus on communicating assertively, this chapter is relevant to the EYP Standards S33–S36, but also to those pertaining to the children, particularly S25–S28, and to families and carers S29–S32.

Introduction

The Common Core of Knowledge and Skills sees assertiveness as a necessary skill for all practitioners if they are to be *proactive, initiate necessary action and be able and prepared to put forward (their) own judgments* (DfES, 2005a, page 18) particularly in multi-agency discussions. As an EYP you have a role in leading discussions and are expected to *explain the rationale for particular changes* and *draw on a repertoire of strategies for inspiring, influencing, and negotiating with others* (CWDC, 2008a, page 5). An understanding of other adults and children is, of course, central to the work but *understanding ourselves* (DfES, 2007a, page 6) and recognising your personal impact is important if you want to engender co-operation and collaboration. Being confident to *implement agreed programmes and interventions on a day-to-day basis* (S36) will depend on how you feel about yourself and how you respond to others.

What do we mean by assertiveness?

Young children can be very assertive, knowing what they want and not being afraid to say so and, because of this, practitioners can find it easy to communicate with them. The communication is straightforward and clear. However, in adult situations, practitioners may find they have lost this ability to say clearly what they mean. This leads to mis-understandings or avoidance of contentious issues and, at worst, conflict. Assertiveness is sometimes equated with dominance and often confused with aggression. Asked for a definition, people will talk about someone who is completely confident, in control and always calm. But how many of us can keep this up all the time? When you are under stress or nervous, although you may not show it outwardly, you can easily lose confidence and this affects the way you communicate. Being assertive does not necessarily take away the anxiety but understanding how your own and others' behaviour affects a situation can help you to handle it better. A positive, energetic presence will inspire others more than a worried, tense one.

Being assertive is primarily about behaving in a way that engenders more open and honest relationships. It requires listening as well as talking. It involves respecting yourself and others and through this developing your self-esteem. You may not necessarily achieve radical changes to organisational frameworks; you are likely to need political means for this. But your personal behaviour can influence the way ideas are taken up, and communicating effectively with others can bring about change. As Pound (2008, page 53) suggests, by *exciting the enthusiasm of other practitioners, both within and beyond the team*, there is the possibility to *transform the self and institution*. There are strategies to be learnt but these have to be combined with self-awareness and an understanding of your own behaviour. Why do you respond to others in certain ways, what patterns of behaviour have you developed, why are some environments easier to communicate in than others? Above all, what are the feelings behind your behaviour that help or inhibit your communication with others? As much as you would like to change others' behaviour, this is not possible; they have to do this themselves. But you can change your own and as a result find people react differently, listening more carefully as they hear you more clearly.

REFLECTIVE TASK

Identify one situation at work or elsewhere where you feel confident and one where you do not feel confident. Try to analyse what it is about these situations that helps or hinders you in your communication. Look, for instance, at the people involved, the context, how you feel about yourself in these situations.

What sort of behaviour?

The situations we find ourselves in can easily affect our behaviour negatively or positively and you may find yourself reacting differently in what seem similar contexts. For example, you may have no trouble speaking to your immediate colleagues, but putting your point over to a specialist or Ofsted inspector, you find yourself getting tongue-tied. In a large meeting you may find your heart beating significantly faster, while you talk much quicker or louder than usual. You may feel confident and enjoy responding to a challenge in some circumstances; in others you may feel fearful. Some situations may remind you of times when you felt intimidated. Past experience may also push you into old patterns of behaviour. For example, you may find it hard to ask someone to help because you have never asked before and feel you should be able to do it yourself. You may not like to say no because you were brought up to be always helpful or not cause trouble. Thus feelings about yourself and others will affect the way you respond.

It is important to recognise that situations you find easy may be difficult for others and vice versa. Some practitioners, for example, say they find it difficult to communicate with older or long-standing members of staff or those with more qualifications, or are nervous when they are called upon to speak up in a group. A group of general practitioners (GPs), confident in their surgeries, when asked at an assertiveness course where and why they had difficulties, came up with very similar ideas to what your team members will probably say:

- feeling intimidated and getting flustered and therefore seeing myself as stupid;

- questioning someone who has more qualifications;

- feeling I am not being taken seriously by colleagues;

- wanting to be liked but having to set boundaries with others;

- expressing a point of view clearly;

- coping with others' aggression;

- managing difficult people;

- dealing with my own anxiety.

Managing feelings

Some feelings are instinctive and prepare our body for 'fight' or 'flight'. Others are developed through our experience. Thus you may find yourself responding aggressively to someone who behaves aggressively towards you, or feel frightened and allow the person to dominate. In either instance, any genuine communication will be difficult. Being able to identify why you are responding in a certain way is the first step to becoming more assertive. You can begin to think of alternatives for dealing with the situation and stop blaming yourself for reacting in a way you do not like. Behaving assertively does not stop the feelings; you may still feel nervous when you have to address a large multi-agency meeting, and irritated when you have to remind unenthusiastic colleagues about putting plans into action. But by recognising that these feelings are an innate part of you, you will manage them so they do not get in the way of the communication. It takes courage to be assertive in certain situations but if you are clear of your role and responsibilities and develop a belief in this and in yourself personally, you will not only raise your own self-esteem but also help others to listen and understand you.

CASE STUDY

1 Patsy has become increasingly irritated by her colleague Andrea who always finds 'more important things to do' when it is time to tidy up at the end of the day, and is generally unhelpful. She finds it difficult to approach her because she has seen her 'bite the head off' another more senior colleague when she suggested she did something differently. As time goes on, Patsy avoids her colleague as much as possible and becomes increasingly unhappy in her work.

2 Mandy also works with Patsy and she too finds Andrea difficult, so if something needs doing she always asks Patsy. She starts her requests with 'you wouldn't mind, would you Patsy', and sometimes 'you're so good at . . .' and Patsy usually does what she's asked.

3 Andrea is clear about what she will and will not do. She comes and goes on time and if asked to do anything extra replies: 'you can't ask me to do that, it's not in my job description'. Most staff avoid her but she is a powerful presence and, particularly when things go wrong, gathers a group round her to complain and blame others.

You may recognise these characters, and they illustrate the way different behaviours affect the communication and also individual feelings. Patsy's passive behaviour is perhaps understandable but it leaves her powerless and nothing changes; Andrea is not an easy person but by avoiding her and not resolving the conflict, Patsy's self-esteem has diminished and, in the long run, her health could be affected. Mandy's relationship with Patsy is not good either. She manipulates Patsy so she will not refuse her requests. This is a form of aggression and could also be seen as subtle bullying. Mandy recognises that she is putting upon Patsy and it leaves her feeling bad. Andrea appears to get what she wants and to know her rights but this type of aggression is detrimental to her relationships with other colleagues. They may feel her power, and in the short term she may be able to dominate them, but it is likely that her aggression breeds aggression from others at work and elsewhere and she spends a lot of her time being angry and unhappy.

Passive behaviour like Patsy's means avoiding the situation or putting oneself down. Simply being frightened may of course result in not taking action. But practitioners who recognise themselves behaving passively often confess that it seems the easy option in difficult situations. In reality, they find themselves powerless and may either be trampled on, ignored or find others feeling sorry for them and/or less respectful. They may use statements such as *I know I'm stupid but . . .* for fear of looking foolish or embarrassed. Vague replies to requests – such as, *I'm not sure, maybe, perhaps* – avoid taking on responsibility or putting oneself in the spotlight. Acting passively with *I don't mind, what do you think* may appear to be a way of pleasing, whereas in reality, the person on the receiving end often becomes irritated and may respond aggressively or take no notice. Nevertheless, this behaviour may stem from a childhood pattern of behaviour, cultural tradition or belief that this is a way of being polite.

You can become frustrated if you remain in a passive position for a long time and this can precipitate aggression. Having waited and not done anything, the person suddenly moves into action, not stopping to think of others or the consequent results. There is a fine line between aggressiveness and assertiveness. Andrea, as you saw, in the short term, appears to get results. She says what she thinks but to the detriment of others' feelings and she does not listen to them. Unlike the passive person who wants to keep out of any trouble, the aggressive may not care. But ultimately, the aggressor may become isolated or not listened to as others avoid him or her. Back and Back (2005) suggest that organisations where there is a culture of aggression can lose talented and inquiring people who are not prepared to work in such an atmosphere. The result is that the staff remaining do not take initiative and dare not rock the boat for fear of reprisals.

Aggression can be loud and offensive but perhaps the most common way it manifests itself in Early Years settings is quiet manipulation. You saw how Mandy manipulated Patsy. Manipulative behaviour plays on others' goodwill or weaknesses. It may appear to be asking others to make their own decisions but ultimately it is a way of getting your own way. You only ask those who you think will respond positively or whom you feel like you. A passive person can also become manipulative if they use their 'helplessness' to get others to do things for them. But very often these actions result in others' resentment as they begin to feel put upon or see others evading responsibility. We all behave non-assertively at times and for many reasons, including those discussed above, but it is important to recognise the consequences of your own behaviour and others'. An important aspect of assertive behaviour is not to blame yourself or others.

A team where people are assertive does not mean that everyone necessarily agrees, but they are open to discussions about difficult issues. A team with a large number of non-assertive practitioners will find it hard to discuss equably and may well have hidden agendas that inhibit decision making or true consensus. The loudest voices often make the decisions as others follow them. Passive members may well always look to others to take the initiative, and the more aggressive will blame others when things go wrong. To change patterns of behaviour, you first have to look at your own behaviour.

REFLECTIVE TASK

Look at the following situations and consider what you do and how you feel when you are faced with them. Try to identify what it is about the situation that makes you behave like this and whether you respond assertively, aggressively or passively. Consider if particular people or situations affect your behaviour. Do not make judgments about yourself. There are no right or wrong answers.

- *You disagree with the way someone is working with a child/young person.*

- *You don't understand what people in a meeting are talking about.*

- *You have asked someone to carry out a job and it has not been done.*

- *You would like help with something but don't want to appear inadequate.*

- *You work with someone who continually complains or moans.*

- *You make a suggestion and no-one takes any notice.*

During a training session at an Early Years setting, staff were asked to identify small tensions or difficulties that arose during the day that they had never admitted before. These were written down anonymously at first and they were assured that nothing was considered too trivial. As people began to discuss these issues, they became more confident and there was a palpable sense of relief and also laughter by the end. Even those who appeared confident to others confessed that there were things they found difficult. Being assertive is not just about being able to say the words; to be able to be honest and open, you also need to believe in yourself and feel that others will listen. Patsy, above, who attended a course on assertive communication, because of the difficulties she was having, learnt some assertive skills and realised:

> *. . . it is not about acting; it is about believing in myself. I have learnt to put across my point of view though I still find it very difficult with some people. I am much more confident in speaking up now. Things that I thought were silly to worry about, I realise can grow into enormous issues. It is better to bring these into the open than leave them to fester. I am quite amazed at the way people treat me differently and I feel so much better about myself and am really enjoying my work with the children now. It's had a knock-on effect on my life outside too because I am so much happier.*

Preparing to put your point across

It can be a risk, or even a new experience, to ask the team to do something or put your point across straightforwardly. Some practitioners find it helpful to remember their role and responsibilities by imagining themselves putting on their 'professional hat'. Much communication is dispersed because it is muddled or unclear, and thinking about what you want to say and to whom is vital. Once you are clear about the objective of your communication then you want to make it as effective as possible. Ask yourself the following questions:

- *WHY am I communicating?* What is the purpose, objective? Do I want to give information, receive information, must I negotiate? How far do I want to go? Is it enough for people to hear my message or do I want them to go away and think about it, accept it or act upon it? People may not fall at your feet and agree with all you say just because you are being assertive. Sometimes it is enough that people have at least heard what you have said. Then they know what your position is;

- *WHO do I need to tell?* It is easy to avoid talking to the right people or person if we are fearful of the outcomes;

- *WHAT do I hope to achieve by this communication?* What does the receiver already know? What does she or he need to know from me?

- *WHERE is the best place to communicate?* The context will make a big difference to how the message is received. Telling someone what you think after a meeting, where it should have been discussed is too late. Talking to someone in front of others so that they are embarrassed will not get results. If you want to confront someone about something that has happened repeatedly, arrange to talk together before it happens again so that you have time to discuss the issue. For example, Carla was unhappy about the way Jean repeatedly hustled a two year old at lunchtime and wanted to ask her to sit down and talk to him to encourage him to eat. She suggested it once at lunchtime but Jean only did it at that point and fairly unwillingly, as she felt other children needed her help too. A few days later, Carla decided to talk to Jean about the child. She sat down with her and they discussed the child, looking at his needs and placing him at the centre of their conversation in a professional way. Jean did not particularly like hearing what Carla had to say but she did not feel that she was being told off;

- *WHEN is the best time to communicate?* To be taken seriously, you need time. It is unlikely that the recipient will hear you if you tell them when they are concentrating on something else or you do a 'by the way' as you leave. Telling someone on a Friday evening could be disastrous if it is critical or 'bad' news;

- *HOW is the best way of communicating this?* Being prepared and knowing what you want to say helps you to be assertive in communication. Even in a meeting, when you may have little time to prepare what you want to say, thinking about your main points before the words come out of your mouth will be much more effective than talking off the top of your head. Communicating assertively is not only about what you say but how you say it. You may notice that you speak in a 'special' voice to certain people either because of the tension you feel or as you try to please. The body language too can speak louder than the words if you are not prepared. You may be someone who smiles easily and this can be inhibiting when you are trying to get a serious point over. You may unconsciously find yourself wagging a finger, an aggressive sign. Many of us have habits such as fiddling with our hands or rings or putting a hand over our mouth as we speak. Standing over someone can be intimidating. Recognising and acknowledging how you are feeling before you speak can help to prepare you so that you are not giving mixed messages. Being aware of your own strengths and difficulties in speaking up assertively can give you an insight into how others may feel. You then understand better why the communication is not effective.

Unlike aggressive or passive behaviour, which does not allow equal dialogue, assertive behaviour encourages others to reply and is respectful. You can allow for differences but also put your own view across. It is not about winning but about communicating. A key skill is to be specific and, thus, clear in your mind about what you want to say. This is often easier said than done, especially if a situation is complex or misunderstanding has gone on for a long time and there are feelings of resentment. Some situations may seem straightforward to others, but can prove hard for the person asking. Aysha, for example, wanted to ask to come in late for several mornings so she could settle her own child as she started school. She had already had a great deal of time off, because she and her daughter had both been ill previously, and she was extremely nervous about asking again. John was unconfident when asking for further information at staff meetings because he was the only man there and did not like drawing attention to himself. Chris, as the youngest member in her room, found it hard to ask to make changes in the way they arranged the toys in the outside shed. On the surface, these may seem like simple requests but underneath are the feelings of guilt, exclusion and lack of confidence.

You are likely to be dealing with much more complex situations and will need to consider what your specific message is. You may find that people do not hear you at first and you may have to repeat yourself. If it is a difficult situation, the likelihood is you have been considering for some time what you want to say. You may even have discussed it with others. But what you have to say could come as a surprise to others. Repeating your words can give you confidence and stop you being sidetracked or manipulated. Janice tells the story of going to her manager, whom she liked but was slightly in awe of, to suggest a new way of re-organising the activities in her room. She felt nervous about asking because she thought her manager might not agree and she wanted to explain the reasons clearly. On walking into the room, she started her requests immediately. Instead of responding to this, her manager said: *oh, Janice, I really love your skirt, where did you get it?* Although you may know what you want to say, the 'script' is flexible. Communicating assertively entails listening to others' responses. Janice, although put off by her manager's response, acknowledged the remark by 'fielding the response', thanking her but not getting hooked into a discussion about clothes, and coming back to the point she wanted to make. Repeating and keeping on track is particularly important if you feel that you are being manipulated. But whatever the discussion, it is important to acknowledge that you have heard the other person even if you do not agree with them. People are more likely to listen to you if they feel you are listening to them. You may need to negotiate, and you want to do this from an equal position allowing the other person to give their view too.

Being in a senior position, you have the authority to ask people to carry out the agreed plans or policy. To help you be clear when making requests, think about the following:

- avoid inconsequential apologies such as *I do hope you don't mind me asking* or *I'm sorry to ask you this but . . .*;

- ask directly rather than hinting: *I'd like to talk to you today* not *it would be good if we could talk sometime*;

- be clear what you want to ask so you keep the request short, otherwise it is confusing for the other person;

- be straight and honest and avoid playing on others' friendship, goodwill or weaknesses;

- Give a reason for your request but avoid making excuses, justifying yourself or blaming others: *Jane, could you go outside with the children this afternoon? Pat won't be here*, rather than *Pat is away **again** and I have to go to a meeting with the health visitor so I can't take her place.*

There is a possibility that the person may refuse your request and fearing this is often the reason why people do not make their requests in a straightforward way. It is easy to take the refusal personally and, especially if you are in a senior position, this may make you feel you have failed in some way. So it is important to recognise that it is the request that has been refused not you as a person. Jane may have a valid reason for not being able to go outside and you will have to look at alternatives. Or, acknowledging the person's refusal, you may have to discuss why she is not willing to do this, repeating your request, without becoming aggressive or passive in your behaviour.

Taking responsibility for what you say means speaking for yourself. So using statements that begin with *I* show your feelings, your beliefs and opinions without cutting out the possibility that others may see things differently. Preceding such remarks as, *it would be much better* or *you could find it easier if* with *I think* or *as I see it* puts the spotlight on you and allow others a choice in whether they agree with you or not. There is a difference between *you should do it like this* and *you could do it like this*. The *could* recognises that there is a possibility of choice. Your role is to give advice but your experience is unique to you, and each person feels and behaves differently. Giving them a choice means that you do not overwhelm someone with your opinion or your expertise. Nevertheless, they also have to take responsibility for the choice they make.

Notice the difference between these two pieces of advice:

- *Oh I know, that happened to me, Martha's mum is really rude. She calmed down with me. You should do like I did, sit her down and give her a cup of tea. We had a long talk;*

- *Yes, I found Martha's mum rude too. I suggest you let her talk and get things off her mind. I found she appreciated having time to talk and so I sat down with her.*

In the first, you are telling the person how you managed it; they may not find this as 'easy' as you; in the second, you use your own experience to give suggestions on how to handle the situation. Chapter 7 will consider in more detail how to give colleagues advice, particularly when there is a conflict situation.

REFLECTIVE TASK

Choose a situation where you have to make a request at work or put your point across either to an individual or a group. Think about the ways you would communicate assertively and how you would prepare yourself for this.

Refusing requests and setting boundaries

Rodd (2006, page 80) highlights the nurturing quality of Early Years practitioners and the danger of burnout if they are not aware of their own needs. Both for your own sake and for others, there are times when you will need to refuse a request. If you believe that others have choices and a right to refuse, then you will find it easier to say no to them. The same principle applies when you refuse a request as when someone refuses a request from you: it is the request you are refusing not the person. You are likely to find it harder to refuse some people than others; perhaps those more senior to you, those you respect because of their skills or knowledge, people you really like or those you feel dislike you. You may worry that you're letting someone down, the other person might be furious or resent you. You could feel that it is selfish to say no, and perhaps feel guilty. However if you do not refuse clearly, it can be confusing for others, or you can find yourself being put upon. Saying no assertively is about setting boundaries and not about being bolshie!

Back and Back (2005) highlight the fact that your role and responsibilities may limit your right to refuse but that you still have the right to say what the difficulties may be. In the same way, your role may demand that you have to refuse certain requests that are either not reasonable or not possible in the circumstances. Being confident in your role in these situations helps you to be clear about the boundaries you have to set and avoid the kind of manipulation that people may use if you do not give the answer they want to hear. This may come in different forms: the non-assertive pleading or aggression: *oh please, I won't ask again . . .*, or *surely you can change it today . . .* The strategies for saying no clearly are similar to those when you make requests:

When saying no at work, think about your role and responsibility.

1 Listen carefully to the request and notice your instinctive response. Ask yourself whether the request is reasonable. This helps you to know whether you really want to say yes or no.

2 If you are not sure what the request involves, ask for more information. For example, if you are being asked to do something, you may want to know:

   • what you would be expected to do;

   • how much time you will need to give;

   • what sort of commitment it requires.

3 Say no clearly without lots of excuses and apologies. If someone persists or tries to manipulate you, repeat what you have said. Give a simple explanation, if necessary.

4 Acknowledge what the person has said so they know you have heard and understood the request. For example: *I realise you want Fola to help you when you go to the park but she is needed in the room this afternoon and I have already arranged for Emma to go with you.*

5 Try not to blame someone else or make them the excuse: '. . . anyway, Fola went to the park with the children yesterday', but take responsibility for saying no.

If you are not used to saying no clearly, it may seem uncomfortable at first. Yet there will be times when you have to set boundaries, for example, in your role with parents. Particularly when parents trust you, it can be hard to tell them where your level of involvement has to end. Giving 'bad' news, even if done assertively, can still leave us with feelings of guilt or anxiety, but managing these is easier if we know that we have communicated honestly, without putting others down.

Rights and responsibilities

Writers on assertiveness (Dickson, 1982; Alberti and Emmons, 2008; Back and Back, 2005) emphasise the importance of knowing your 'rights'. As Back and Back (2005) suggest, and as the case of Andrea above illustrated, this may seem to imply an aggressive insistence on them. But assertive behaviour allows you to exercise these rights without denying others theirs and gives you confidence if you have something difficult to communicate. You will communicate with each on an equal level. The 1989 United Nations Convention on the Rights of the Child (UNCRC) upholds the rights of children, and the Children Act 2004 and *Every Child Matters* promote the views and interests of children. Some children will find it difficult to exercise their rights, and adults will need to help them experience and understand these as well as help them understand the responsibilities that go with them (Kinney, 2005). Adults who understand their personal rights and responsibilities will find this easier. The rights below are based on those enshrined in law and your personal rights as a human being. They are not inclusive but a starting point to think about, and relevant for adults and children. They are also helpful when you are feeling nervous and can ask yourself the question: *can I say this?* Saying the right to yourself before you speak can give you confidence in difficult situations.

REFLECTIVE TASK

Read the following rights (adapted from: Dickson 1982; Back and Back, 2005).

    1   *I have the right to be treated as an equal human being.*

    2   *I have the right to express my feelings.*

    3   *I have the right to give my opinion and say what I believe.*

    4   *I have the right to say No or Yes for myself.*

    5   *I have the right to be human and make mistakes or fail.*

    6   *I have the right to change my mind.*

    7   *I have the right to say I don't know or I don't understand and to ask for more information.*

    8   *I have the right to ask for what I want.*

    9   *I have the right not to take responsibility for other people's problems.*

    10   *I have the right to do things without being dependent on others for approval.*

    11   *I have the right to be myself which may be the same as, or different from, what others would like.*

    12   *I have the right to decide not to assert myself.*

- *Decide whether you agree with the rights above or not and whether you think everyone is entitled to them. You may like to discuss these with your colleagues.*

- *You may find you give others certain rights but not yourself or vice versa. If you do the former this produces passive behaviour, the latter aggressive. Choose one that you feel you do not allow yourself easily and think about its implications.*

REFLECTIVE TASK continued

- *For example, I have the right to make mistakes or fail does not mean that you can be slapdash or careless but it does allow us to forgive others and ourselves when things go wrong. You may find this hard if you are a perfectionist.*

- *Consider how denying yourself the right could affect others. For example, you may find it difficult to say what you believe because you fear being put down. This could lead to passive or aggressive behaviour that will affect the way you communicate with them.*

- *Consider some ways that you can help children and adults to exercise their rights and understand their responsibilities.*

CASE STUDY

Helen is a much-liked and respected EYP in a children's centre. Suzi, who works in a different area to her, corners her in the staff room whenever she can to ask for advice and help. Helen finds that her break time is being eroded because she spends most of her time listening to Suzi. After a time, she realises what is happening and recognises that she can either spend time supporting Suzi, who certainly needs this, or make the most of a short break in the staff room. She finds it hard to break the pattern but eventually tells Suzi that although she is happy to talk, she also needs a break and that Suzi needs to talk to colleagues in her room or to her line manager about her concerns.

REFLECTIVE TASK

Look at the case study above. Do you think Helen is right to withdraw her support from Suzi? Do you think she can support her in any other way? How would Helen give this piece of information to Suzi:

- *passively;*

- *manipulatively;*

- *aggressively;*

- *assertively?*

Now ask yourself the following questions and write down your responses:

- *what might be the consequences of Helen behaving in any of these ways?*

- *how do you think Helen and Suzi might feel after this conversation?*

- *what would be the best way for Helen to end the conversation?*

Being assertive is not learnt overnight and if you have difficulty, say, in getting your point across, it may take you some time to feel confident to do so. The best way to become more assertive is to first become aware of your behaviour and how this is affecting the communication. Then begin to practise being assertive in what feels like the least difficult situations. Reflecting afterwards on the reasons you put your viewpoint over clearly, or not, will help you to be realistic about your behaviour and not blame yourself if you are not totally successful. Assertiveness comes with practice.

C H A P T E R   S U M M A R Y

This chapter has discussed some of the basic skills for being assertive. It has identified passive, aggressive and assertive behaviour and exemplified how these can affect communication between colleagues. It has given you some strategies for putting your point of view over assertively. It stressed that feelings are a natural part of us and have to be managed, not denied, in difficult situations, as they can affect the way we communicate verbally and non-verbally.

Moving on

The next chapter begins with some discussion about what is meant by collaboration in its fullest sense. It continues the theme of effective communication in teams, looking at ways to promote forums where practitioners find it easy to communicate openly and confidently with each other. It offers some practical ways for making group meetings more effective and inclusive.

Self-assessment exercise

Look at a situation where you have to put your point of view, make a request or set boundaries. Use the following questions to help you.

1 What is the message that you want to get across? When you are clear, how can you be specific? What do you want to accomplish in your communication?

2 Consider the feelings you have about dealing with this situation.

3 Identify the ingredients in the situation that are impacting on your feelings, e.g. the people, the context, never having done this before, the pressure to do this right.

4 What negative messages are you giving to yourself? *For example I'm going to look foolish; nobody is going to support me on this; it won't come out right; so-and-so is going to be very upset.*

5 How can you reverse this negative talk – e.g. *the worst that could happen to me is . . .?*

6 Now you have recognised your feelings, how can you manage them so they don't get in the way of the communication? Here are some suggestions to help you:

a notice and acknowledge to yourself that you feel like this and that you may shake or blush then concentrate on what you have to say;

b if appropriate, acknowledge verbally to others that you feel like this. *I feel anxious . . .; I feel upset . . .*, then concentrate on what you have to say;

c be aware that you may need to physically release these feelings afterwards by going for a walk, taking some deep breaths and relaxing, playing a game with the children.

7   Looking at the rights above, which ones could give you confidence to act assertively?

8   What will you do if the others ask questions or do not immediately take on your suggestion?

9   What would be a satisfactory and realistic outcome for you?

a they hear what you have to say even if they do not immediately act on it;

b you have a discussion about it;

c they agree to do something about it;

d you change the world!

10 If you are not totally successful this time in your communication, how will you learn from it?

11 If you are successful in your communication, how will you learn from it?

12 Are you ready to try communicating assertively?

FURTHER READING

Back, K, Back, K (2005) *Assertiveness at work: a practical guide to handling awkward situations*, 3rd edition. Maidenhead: McGraw-Hill.

Dickson, A (1982) *A woman in your own right*. London: Quartet Books.

5 Meeting together: creating listening forums

CHAPTER OBJECTIVES

In the last chapter, we looked at the EYP's role as a key communicator in the team and this chapter looks at ways of creating an ethos for collaborative and co-operative working so that groups of staff feel able to speak up and give their ideas in a safe environment. The latter half of the chapter considers practical strategies for constructing effective meetings: the purpose and organisation, the roles of the members and how EYPs can take an active part as either leader or member of a meeting.

After reading this chapter, you should be able to:
*   discuss ways of creating an environment where staff can communicate honestly and openly;
*   analyse the effectiveness of the meetings you attend;
*   reflect on the different roles you take on in a meeting.

This chapter focuses on all the EYP Standards for Teamwork and Collaboration (S33–36) and also makes reference to the way you communicate with parents (S30) and the importance of developing your professional role (S38).

Introduction

The EYFS practice guide expects practitioners to *work collaboratively within the setting to share knowledge, question practice and test new ideas – with high aspirations for every child* (DCSF, 2008c, page 9). Collaboration is at the heart of the government's drive for agencies to work together. The Common Assessment Framework, for example, where services are obliged to co-operate and communicate with each other can even be seen as *enforced collaboration* (McCullogh, 2007, page 32). The concept of 'collaboration' is often used in a vague way. Definitions range from getting together with someone informally to a much longer-term commitment. Mercer and Littleton's (2007) research is focused on children collaborating together, but it is equally relevant to adults. They suggest that collaboration can happen by chance but that it is more than just co-operating or interacting; it involves 'interthinking' and requires:

. . . a coordinated joint commitment to a shared goal, reciprocity, mutuality and the continual (re)negotiation of meaning.

(Mercer and Littleton, 2007, page 25)

What does collaboration look like?

Collaborating together engenders a 'groupsense' where participants value their contributions and understand the common goal. Reciprocity allows those involved to share ideas and to have these valued. For instance, parents', children's or practitioners' viewpoints may not coincide but this is recognised, respected, discussed and used creatively to learn together. Power relationships begin to shift (Rodd, 2006) as those involved begin to listen to each other and understand each other's position. Mutuality involves a common cause or concern; thus, keeping the child at the centre of discussion and decision making helps those collaborating to move towards a common goal. If services are to collaborate then it is incumbent on all practitioners to look at how they can improve and enhance what they offer (French, 2007). The five outcomes of *Every Child Matters* are common to all children's services, and a child- and family-centred approach is a basic premise. This may not mean that practitioners agree on how to accomplish such a service but it lays down a common starting point from which to collaborate. A great advantage of collaborating is that it is an effective way of making the most of a range of knowledge and expertise and that organisations, speaking with a united voice will be heard more easily and gain respect from the policy makers (Rodd, 2006). And Mercer and Littleton (2007) suggest that it is when tasks are complex, and where no-one has the complete answer that the most successful collaboration often takes place.

With the drive towards more integrated services, *joined-up thinking* was a phrase that was prevalent in the nineties. But to be able to think together, you need to be able to understand each other. This is crucial within multidisciplinary teams where the vocabulary used has originated from different professional training and is an integral part of the culture. Anning *et al* (2006) suggest that acronyms are often used to create a smoke screen, and jargon can be a way of defending status when services do not trust or understand each other's role and responsibilities. Within your core team, you may find that staff have either not had practice in discussing issues that are commonplace to you, or do not even share the same language. This does not mean 'talking down' to others, but avoiding jargon and using a language that is universal. As an EYP, you can role model this by checking others' understanding, acknowledging what has been said or asked, and asking the kind of questions that enhance the discussion. It takes time, particularly in a multidisciplinary team, or indeed with parents, to build the kind of relationships where everyone feels confident enough to ask questions or say they do not understand.

Allowing opportunities for people to ask for explanations when they don't understand, or discussing issues where no-one has an easy answer, and allowing others to admit this too, goes a long way to developing a collaborative approach. As a more qualified member of the team, it is easy to feel that you should know the answer and you can find yourself steering the group to what you think is the right way. Van Oers and Hännikäinen (2001) emphasise the need to develop relationships where you feel confident enough to go on discussing even when the going gets tough. Collaboration allows disagreements but those involved *feel obliged to each other, stay with each other and maintain togetherness* (Van Oers and Hännikäinen, 2001, page 105).

Our obligation to each other is for the children. As Early Years practitioners, wherever you work, there is a responsibility to improve the child's 'well-being'. This involves their *physical and mental health and emotional well-being; protection from harm and neglect; education, training and recreation* (Childcare Act, 2006, page 1). The responsibilities may vary but Early Years practitioners are all in this together. Relationships with each other do not need to be close but they do need to be respectful and understood.

REFLECTIVE TASK

Think of some occasions where you:

- *are working collaboratively with children;*

- *are working collaboratively with other adults;*

- *feel you are moving towards a more collaborative approach with other adults.*

What do you think are the conditions that allow this to happen?

Developing safe forums

Regular forums are necessary if practitioners are to understand and appreciate their own and others' contributions and share knowledge and good practice (Clark and Moss, 2001). Even a brief meeting every day creates a culture where communicating with each other is seen as a central part of the work. The Reggio Emilia nurseries build in 6 of their 36 weekly working hours as non-contact time with the children. This time is set aside for a daily dialogue with other staff and parents and for weekly meetings. Best practice, as demonstrated by international research can only develop if practitioners have opportunities for ongoing discussions (MacNaughton, 2005). It is not enough for practitioners to listen to children and document what they observe; they need to reflect on and interpret their observations with other adults to extend their understanding of the children (Rinaldi, 2006). To do this, communication needs to be seen as an important tool, both as a means of support and as a way of learning together with any time spent together used productively. In the next chapter we look more closely at the way teams can develop as learning communities, but here we look at the practicalities needed to create a place where people feel safe to talk. If communicating together is an issue in your setting, start by talking about the best ways of doing this; consider some of the systems discussed in Chapter 3. Then look at some of the skills needed.

The DfES (2007a, page 1) in its advice on working collaboratively with other organisations recommends the following:

- discussions about strategies for moving forward should be open, transparent and inclusive. It is through the day-to-day interaction in settings that dilemmas are worked out;

- professionals need to feel psychologically safe in organisations in order to take risks. We need to create safe spaces and forums for workers to share, discuss and debate issues that are important to them;

- organisations which support children's care, learning and development must develop a culture of collaboration;

- meaningful change comes through development of self-awareness and development of trusting relationships between colleagues, both within settings and between organisations and the communities they serve. Putting this into practice in your core group will go a long way to helping staff feel confident when talking to professionals outside their workplace.

REFLECTIVE TASK

1 *From reading the DfES advice, how far do you feel your setting has created safe spaces and forums for workers to share, discuss and debate issues that are important to them?*

2 *Having considered this, ask yourself where and with whom you feel most confident in your communication and why this is. For example:*

- *one-to-one;*

- *small working groups;*

- *larger staff meetings;*

- *with parents and visitors to the setting;*

- *with other professionals outside the workplace.*

3 *Now think about where the other members in your team display most confidence when communicating.*

You may find that practitioners feel confident in one-to-one communication or talking to specific people but find it hard to reflect on and discuss their personal and professional beliefs in other circumstances. The pressure in Early Years settings to 'perform' often means that staff are looking at 'what next' rather than taking time to reflect on what they have already done and building on this. Acknowledging what you don't know, especially if you have worked for a long time, may feel risky. Similarly, as someone who may have had experience elsewhere but is new to Early Years practice, some questions may seem too obvious to ask.

CASE STUDY

Maggie, an EYP, described two small planning teams she attends in her centre and examined the reason why one was blossoming and the other not. She found that within one there was a willingness to be open. The team had worked together for some time and developed a friendship base and trust in each other. The team members were good practitioners but had had little experience in analysing or reflecting on what they were doing. With Maggie's encouragement and input they had come to the point where they were ready to 'fly'. The other team, also good practitioners and, in fact, with more qualifications, were reluctant to speak up; the support for each other was missing. The man in the group was new to Early Years and was still finding his feet. He found it hard to put his ideas across in a group with very strong and experienced women. Another, though an excellent practitioner, had not reached the stage where she could recognise or acknowledge her own abilities. Instead of being positive about the team's achievements, she tended to complain about minor things that were not working.

Democratic professionalism, a concept referred to in Chapter 3, implies participation and *collaborative, cooperative action between professional colleagues* (Oberheumer, 2005, page 13). This presupposes that there is a feeling of equality amongst practitioners. But, as Maggie's experience shows, this may take time to develop and it can be a challenge for practitioners, even those who have completed courses and gained qualifications, to develop the kind of knowledge base where they feel able to contribute to discussions. Some may know the theory, others the practice. When practitioners feel unconfident about their knowledge and cannot communicate their dilemmas or uncertainties with each other, what hope have they of communicating well with the children and their families? In your role as a 'reflective practitioner' (CWDC, 2008a, page 5), even in short daily meetings you can encourage reflection on what you as a team have already done and how you can develop this. You can share and compare concerns and ideas and ask for and give information and search for answers together. Your one-to-one discussions may entail reassurance or support but are also important for pooling knowledge about the children.

REFLECTIVE TASK

Creating a listening forum for groups to communicate
In the light of your experience in your past or present work:

- *what is needed for people to feel they can talk openly with each other?*

- *how does the space or forum impact on communication?*

- *who or what do you think helps develop trusting, respectful relationships?*

- *what can you do to develop forums where staff feel confident to discuss issues openly with each other?*

Group meetings

Much of the communication that takes place may happen informally, perhaps in the staff room or as you work together with the children. And it can be difficult to find opportunities to meet as a team because of shift patterns, different hours of work or cover for staff. You may attend meetings that comprise a large or small number of people in formal and informal environments. Informality does not necessarily bring good communication. With limited time available, meetings are precious and therefore need to be purposeful and productive with *maximum member engagement* (Garmston, 2005, page 65). In financial terms, meetings can be costly too. If you consider the salaries, administrative and possible travel costs and refreshments, of say, a multi-agency meeting, you are likely to come up with a large sum. Most people have learnt the ways to behave in meetings through attending them and yet there are actual skills to be learnt which they may never have discussed. When the meeting is poor or chaotic, the person chairing or facilitating often gets the blame. He or she should certainly take some responsibility but the other members also have a role to play in keeping the meeting focused.

The style of any meeting will depend on its purpose and its members. If procedures are not made clear beforehand, then things are likely to go wrong. For example, some parents invited to meetings may have had little experience of them. They can find it difficult to speak up or, not used to the 'formal' nature of a meeting, interrupt continually. The framework is there to give opportunities for everyone to give their view. If not introduced to the norms of a meeting beforehand, some parents can find themselves in an invidious position – either not listened to because they say nothing or appear aggressive because they interrupt. Well-run and organised meetings with a clear framework, even if quite formal, create safe forums where people can share ideas. Ground rules or norms that have been established beforehand act as a safety net, so people feel free to discuss differences or to ask questions. Knowing why you have been invited to the meeting helps you to understand your role within it. Are you expected to contribute or merely be a spectator? Discussions about matters that do not concern or exclude members or that are unfocused can create a cynicism that may colour their feelings about meetings as a whole.

CASE STUDY

Dee and Selina used to attend two meetings for Extended Services. Finding that the same people attended both and there was much duplication, these merged into one that is now focused and effective. The chairperson takes an independent position but is knowledgeable about the services in the area. He steers the meeting, reiterates what has been said and clarifies if necessary but does not dominate. The meeting includes information sharing and five-minute slots for describing good practice. All members can contribute to the agenda and there are definite terms of reference for attending the meeting.

Dee and Selina compare this meeting to another they attend for children centre managers. The meeting has been organised so there is an element of training and each time two different members present case studies. They find these pertinent to their job.

The rest of the agenda's content they consider a waste of their time and they do not have any input into it. They complain: 'the meeting's organisers give us what they think we need, but the information is either out of date or too far in advance to be relevant'.

REFLECTIVE TASK

Consider the meetings you attend and think about why some are effective and others are not.

Use the following questions to help you:

- *does the meeting have a clear purpose?*
- *do the right people attend the meeting?*
- *is there an appropriate leadership style?*
- *is there a clear and organised agenda?*
- *do the members at the meeting remain focused?*

When you have considered these questions, decide on one or two ways for improving the meeting and if there is any action you could take to do this.

Why meet?

You may meet for a number of reasons but all participants need to be clear of the common purpose or goal. Most importantly they need to understand the nature of their contributions and the limits of their decision-making authority (Delehant, 2007).

The agenda is important in reflecting this. Your meetings generally involve planning, monitoring and evaluating, although not necessarily every time, and you will need time for sharing information, looking at problems and ways of solving these and making decisions. Marking items on the agenda to show whether they are for general discussion or decision making can help members focus. The meeting time should also be an opportunity for team building where members give and receive support, look at and resolve differences and feel a sense of involvement.

Regular meetings can become such routine events that participants take them for granted and they lose their purpose. It is also easy for meetings to become totally task orientated or focused on the outcomes. That is, you only look at what and how you carry out the work. Meetings are also important for members' professional development and for building effective teams, and if only concerned with giving information will not address this. You considered the importance of fostering the group needs in Chapter 2, and a major reason for meeting is to make sure individuals do not become isolated. There are opportunities to reflect on what has gone before and how the work is developing. Particularly if time is an issue or when success is mainly measured by the outcomes, the process is not always understood or valued (Rinaldi, 2006). If no attention is given to the process and discussions about it are neglected, there is no opportunity to develop practice.

REFLECTIVE TASK

After you have attended your next meeting, reflect on how much of it focused on the task and how much attention was given to the process. Consider whether the ratios were correct for that particular meeting. Was enough time spent on the tasks that had to be discussed and how was the time allocated so the group felt involved in the discussions together?

Preparing for meetings

The preparation for a meeting is just as important as its execution, and what happens beforehand will go a long way towards its success. Having an agenda in advance, however informal, allows people to prepare their thoughts and questions. Knowing exactly when the meeting starts and finishes gives a focus. The environment will influence the way the meeting goes, and although it is sometimes difficult to find an ideal place, it needs to be conducive to discussion and the room arranged so that people feel able to contribute. Even a simple change to the furniture arrangement and places where people sit can influence how the meeting proceeds. It is easy for people to come to regular meetings like homing pigeons, always sitting in the same seat. This may be because they want to avoid attention or, conversely, want to dominate. People with less power in the organisation may avoid sitting near those who have more. The physical position of the participants is often indicative of the power relations within the group and the way they communicate together is also a good indicator of how a team is working.

CASE STUDY

Sarah was new to a senior management team in her local authority and when attending meetings found that she was always placed on a corner of the table where she could be overlooked. The others sat in the same place at each meeting and Sarah noticed definite alliances in the way they did this. After a few meetings, she recognised why she was finding it difficult to get her point of view across. She decided to go to the next meeting earlier than the others and sat herself in a new position. There was general discomfiture when the others arrived but it looked childish to say 'that's my place' so the arrangement changed. The meeting changed for Sarah too.

Timing

The time of day and the conditions in which the meeting take place will have a profound effect on the level of communication. When the meeting is at the end of the day, some staff may always make for the easy chairs. This could indicate the way they perceive the meeting. Good communication within meetings demands concentration and alertness; it is a tall order to expect all staff to be decisive or receptive at the end of the day. Appropriate conditions and preparation for the meeting allow members to move into a 'zone of receivership' so that they are more likely to listen and participate (Smith and Langston,1999, page 88). Tropman (1996) highlights the way the shape of the meeting affects participation. The meeting progresses from the easier items through the most difficult to the easiest ones at the end. At the beginning of the meeting, members usually need a settling period; busy staff require time to re-focus; they may be coming from a phone call with a parent, another meeting or an upset child. Film directors or playwrights rarely put the most important words at the beginning of a play because an audience takes time to settle and concentrate; similarly members of meetings need time to bring their attention to the matters discussed. Tropman (1996) suggests that the middle third of the meeting is when participants' physical focus, physiological alertness, attention and attendance are at their sharpest. Thus, it is at this point that their concentration and ability to make decisions are at their greatest. As the meeting comes to the end, their attention may slip as they begin preparing psychologically – or even physically – for what is to come afterwards: going home, another meeting, returning to the children. Having a clear beginning and end and asking people to commit to this time also gives a shape to the meeting. Interruptions, as people come in late, can disrupt the flow of thought and discussion; going over the time allotted, unless agreed with the participants, is another way of losing their attention and, indeed, their goodwill.

The framework for the meeting

Preparing an agenda, even for short meetings or one-to-one meetings, gives it purpose and focus. There is never time to discuss everything so it will mean prioritising. This may appear to formalise the proceedings but if prepared beforehand, it allows people to think about the issues, understand the reasons for the meetings and structure the discussions. It acts as a map, pointing the meeting in the right direction if it is used as an efficient rather than bureaucratic tool (Goldschmied and Jackson, 2004). Who puts this agenda together and how they do this will also have a considerable effect on how participants react to or discuss issues. For instance, if the manager always draws up the agenda, then participants in the meeting will not feel any sense of ownership. Practitioners not used to being involved in contributing may need encouragement. You may need to approach individuals beforehand and discuss with them what they would like to see on the agenda. Meetings can develop into forums for directives or instructions if not handled carefully, an easy trap for managers, particularly when there are staff who neither seem to respond nor actively take part in meetings, is to make the agenda into a list of information. Some staff groups create an agenda with the standard headings. There is a danger with this format that the meeting becomes boring and repetitive and there is no room for creative thinking.

The agenda mirrors the purpose of the meeting. What are the issues up for discussion, do you need to take decisions, consult over a new idea, plan for the future? Delehant (2007) suggests that as well as understanding what is on the agenda, it is important for people to understand the *non-purpose* of the meeting. This defines the boundaries. There will be certain issues that are not relevant for the meeting. For example, sometimes members absent at the previous meeting want to go over what was said before. The minutes will sum up what was said and should be discussed at the beginning but their purpose is not to re-run the last meeting. There may be items on the agenda for decision making, but these may be within certain parameters. For instance, practitioners may not agree with a decision that has come, say, from the local authority or the nursery owner, but their role is to look at how to put this into practice, not to spend the meeting complaining about a decision that has already been made.

Well-organised meetings create a safe forum for discussions. You may not want to go over the ground rules every time you meet, but it is a good idea to discuss them at some point and come back to them from time to time. It reminds participants about the importance of confidentiality and the need to speak respectfully about children and their families and to each other. Knowing that everyone is respected and valued allows people to offer differing views without feeling they will be put down or not listened to.

REFLECTIVE TASK

Have you discussed ground rules within your group meetings or do you have tacit agreements? Are members of your meetings clear about:

- *timing?*
- *confidentiality?*
- *active listening?*
- *using differences positively?*
- *roles and responsibilities in the meeting?*

Playing your part at meetings

Tropman (1996) uses the metaphor of a good orchestra to illustrate a successful meeting. There is a suitable venue and the orchestra has rehearsed; the players understand their responsibility to do their best, knowing that their contribution adds to the whole effect even if they only play a few notes; the conductor keeps time and manages the dynamics. Taking part in a meeting involves contributing as an individual, but also taking account of the group. To make decisions together, there needs to be mutuality, and at the same time, a possibility to bring in individual ideas. The person facilitating the meeting can do much to help participation, but if the participants understand their rights and responsibilities, they can contribute with confidence. Members frequently invest the chairperson with rights so that the meeting can progress, but they do not always see themselves as having rights (Back and Back, 2005). Setting ground rules beforehand and developing norms together can assist members in recognising their rights and responsibilities. A group of practitioners wanted to improve their meetings and after discussion came up with a set of ground rules based on Back and Back's (2005) suggestions for participants' rights in meetings:

We will:

- *start and finish the meeting on time;*
- *find out the purpose of the meeting before it starts;*
- *give our opinions or suggestions;*
- *ask questions if we don't understand;*
- *listen to each other and respond;*
- *say if we disagree with another's point of view or suggestions;*
- *use the meetings effectively and not waste time going over old ground;*
- *avoid interruptions and consider the meeting as the priority for that time.*

REFLECTIVE TASK

Consider the ground rules above and mark any that you feel are relevant to your meetings. Add any others that you would like to see there. Then consider whether your meetings allow members these rights or if you allow yourself these rights. For instance, although you may agree that it is the right of members to understand what is going on and you have the right to ask questions, how easy do you find this in large meetings or ones where there are specialists or people with a different knowledge base from you? Think also about how others in your team exercise their rights.

When you have considered the rights, look at the responsibilities that people need to take on to exercise these within a group.

You may have the right to speak up in a meeting but so do others. Thinking about what you want to say before you say it, keeping it short and to the point and saying it at the relevant time means that people are more likely to hear you. Making sure you say it to everyone by looking round at them means that they feel included. Some nervous members of your group will need encouragement to do this; often people carry a history with them, making judgments on themselves or on others when they speak. There may be members of your team who find it difficult to speak up, possibly, as you considered in the last chapter, because of their previous experience. Speaking up at a meeting may bring memories of answering questions at school or feeling foolish at another meeting, but their views are as valid as others' and they may need help to give these. As an EYP in the team, you can act as a useful voice both feeding back information from other meetings and sometimes speaking on a small group's behalf.

'Groupthink'

Janis (1972) adopted the term groupthink, suggesting that it occurs principally in groups that do not want to consider differences and therefore make faulty decisions. He gave examples of political decisions occurring because of this and their devastating affects. Groupthink frequently occurs in Early Years teams: in the 'cosy' team (Edgington, 2004) where the group is inward looking and has not learned to take a 'critical' look at its work; in teams that do not want to be challenged; and in teams where differences could disturb the status quo. With the pressure for, and rapidity of change in Early Years, it is not surprising that some groups prefer to stay with what they know. Groupthink is especially damaging in decision making when members do not want to examine alternatives for working with children or parents, holding on to stereotypes or negative, past experiences. A strong or charismatic leader or dominant member in the meeting can engender groupthink as others follow their lead. There may also be small cliques who groupthink and exclude themselves from the larger group. Very often these groups cling together because of lack of confidence, although this may appear as aggressiveness. An EYP suggested that practitioners within her setting working with families in distress often experienced strong emotions but had to contain these when supporting them. If they were not able to express these emotions elsewhere, this brought a volatility or unpredictability to the group discussions.

It is a good idea to divide people up in small groups or pairs in the meeting sometimes, so there is a different structure for discussing more contentious issues. It is worth looking at some different exercises for doing this in training materials; you will see some practical ideas in the recommended reading for this chapter. Although a cohesive group is a positive asset, it is important to make sure that there are opportunities to look at alternatives, evaluate what has been achieved and encourage people to look objectively at their work. You may have to act as devil's advocate sometimes, asking difficult questions or suggesting ways of looking at things in a different way. Practitioners who come in from other services can also be helpful in offering new ways of thinking or, indeed, asking uncomfortable questions.

The meeting in action

In some settings, the most senior members of the group tend to take the lead in the meeting. But this can be inhibiting to the group who may confuse the role of the person chairing or facilitating the meeting with their role as manager. The leader too can be put in a difficult position as people look to them for the answers and the more the leader speaks, the less other members contribute. There is often a belief amongst members that the person chairing has to know and understand everything. But where people know and trust each other, having opportunities to take on different roles, even if not for the whole meeting, develops their transferable skills such as speaking in public, writing minutes or chairing a group. The chairperson's main role is to keep the meeting focused and facilitate the process and not to spend too much time talking. Where staff are clear about the differing roles in meetings and recognise that everyone has a contribution to make, they will invest the person chairing the meeting with the role and respect their position. Obviously different meetings will demand different styles but there are still skills that are essential wherever you are. Here are some.

Opening and introducing the meeting and establishing the atmosphere

A leader who starts and finishes on time will be much appreciated. The way you begin the meeting, both verbally and with your body language, will have an enormous impact on those in the meeting. You may need to welcome new members and you will need to introduce the agenda, saying what the meeting is for, and referring to the agenda to explain the framework.

Conducting the meeting

The skill here is to allow flexibility but also maintain control so people keep to the point. Your job is to seek people's opinion, clarify points so everyone understands, summarise what has been said, weigh up contributions impartially and help people to reach a decision, where necessary, or conclude a discussion. Particularly where people are new or working in different environments, it is important to listen carefully to the language used. It is easy to make assumptions about what people already know. As chairperson or as a member, you can pick these up and make sure everyone understands what is being discussed. Other members are often extremely grateful when someone is prepared to speak up and ask what something means.

Concluding the meeting

Discussions at the end of meetings can evaporate as people rush off to other places or begin talking to each other. Having a clear and positive statement from the chairperson at the end, summing up what has been discussed, and what may be on the next agenda, gives people a sense of achievement even when they have examined contentious issues or not been able to come to a conclusion. There are many books on making meetings effective, but there is no better way of learning than actually taking part. For colleagues who are nervous about taking the lead, you may like to suggest that they first act as a timekeeper and then move on to chairing one item on the agenda. To delegate to someone else for a particular item where the chairperson has strong opinions and needs to be involved in the discussion can be extremely helpful to everyone.

PRACTICAL TASK

Damaging meetings
This is a useful exercise to do with your team because, although it may not seem serious, it actually draws attention to what can easily happen.

List as many words as you can beginning with D which are ways of or tactics for damaging meetings: for example distracting, deviating, destroying confidence, denying all knowledge.

A group carrying out this task came up with 30 that you will find in Appendix 1 on page 117.

(Sharman, 1993)

After the meeting

Ask for volunteers to take the minutes and there is rarely a rush forward. It is important to reassure people that they do not have to take every word down or tell a story. A chairperson who summarises at the end of each item can help the minute taker to be accurate. Minute takers need to feel they have rights like the members so that they can clarify and understand what is being said. Minutes will depend on the style of the meeting but the clearer and more focused they are the better. Many settings have developed their own way of formatting minutes but you will find an example in Appendix 2 on page 118 of a type of format similar to that used by many settings for their weekly staff meetings. Obviously it is not suitable for some of the more formal meetings you attend. This format clearly shows people's responsibilities, what action needs to be taken and when. Using the minutes to record who is present each time can highlight the absence or lateness of certain members. Clearly, it is sometimes difficult for people to attend the whole meeting or they may only attend the items relevant to them, but if each item is numbered then it is possible to write the absentees against these. Thus you may find that one person rarely arrives until item 3 or another always leaves just before the last. There may be genuine reasons for this, but it also highlights the people who are always late!

Meetings, whether formal or informal, are an integral part of teamwork. They need to be productive not just routine. They may be focused on planning or evaluation or on improving collaboration within the team. But perhaps one of the best ways of judging the meetings you attend, that may vary in their agendas and members, is always to ask the question: how does this meeting support the children and families we work with?

C H A P T E R   S U M M A R Y

This chapter began by considering what collaboration constitutes in its fullest sense. It has highlighted the need to create forums where this can take place and where practitioners can feel confident to speak up and feel psychologically safe to take risks. It suggested that it can take time for people to feel a sense of equality in the group but that the Early Years Professional can be instrumental in developing this.

Moving on

In the next chapter, we consider some of the debates about raising the quality of practice through developing a professional workforce and what being a professional constitutes. We look at your role in the team for supporting individuals in their professional development and ways of reflecting together on the work they do.

Self-assessment exercise

In this chapter, we have looked at some of the ingredients for making meetings effective. Sometimes you will be a member, sometimes chairing. Carry out this self-audit tool and consider what skills you offer and what you need to improve. You might find that you display your skills better in some meetings than others. Think why this is and what you might do to improve them.

Skills as a member of a meeting	Always	Never	Usually/ sometimes	Comment
I state my points clearly and audibly.				
I ask questions if I am not clear.				
I listen carefully to others and show that I am listening.				
I prepare for the meeting beforehand, reading any information that is needed.				
I ask for feedback when I have contributed, if appropriate.				
I say when I disagree and when I agree.				
I am aware of those who are less confident and support them.				
I take what others say seriously.				
I arrive on time for meetings.				

Skills as a chairperson	Always	Never	Usually/ sometimes	Comment
I start and finish the meeting on time.				
I describe the purpose of the meeting and introduce the agenda.				
I discuss ground rules, if appropriate.				
I invite contributions and listen carefully.				

I encourage people to keep to the point.				
I bring the members back to the items under discussion.				
I summarise points made and make sure the minute taker is clear.				
I ask questions and clarify.				
I ask how members feel about the issues under discussion.				
I encourage people to explore new ideas.				
I make it clear when a decision has to be made.				
I check for agreements.				
I remain neutral so that people can discuss different points of view.				

FURTHER READING

Delehant, A (2007) *Making meetings work: how to get started, get going, and get it done.* London: Sage Publications.

6 Developing professional learning together

C H A P T E R   O B J E C T I V E S

This chapter discusses some of the arguments about the meaning of professionalism and asks you to consider what it may look like in Early Years contexts. It considers the concept of 'democratic professionalism', introduced earlier, and its place in Early Years environments. It suggests that professional learning is developed through communities of practice and that collaboration is an essential part of these communities.

After reading this chapter, you should be able to:
- compare different views on the meaning of professionalism;
- understand the nature of a learning community;
- reflect on your role in developing professional learning.

This chapter mainly focuses on the EYP Standards 33 and 34 but is also relevant to the Standards relating to the lead and support you give others to develop effective practice with children, particularly S6, S7, S13 and S24.

Introduction

The government's vision, set out in the 2020 Children and Young People's Workforce Strategy (DCSF, 2008a, page 6) is that everyone working with children and young people will be:

- ambitious for every child and young person;

- excellent in their practice;

- committed to partnership and integrated working;

- respected and valued as professionals.

  The Effective Provision of Preschool Education (EPPE) report (Sylva et al, 2004) concluded that qualified teachers, specifically as pedagogical leaders, had the most impact on the quality of children's experiences, particularly in relation to outcomes in pre-reading and social development. The EYFS Practice Guidance, taking note of this, stresses the need for well-qualified and experienced staff who understand and engage in informed reflective practice – both individually and in groups and work collaboratively within the setting to share knowledge, question practice and test new ideas – with high aspirations for every child.

(DCSF, 2008c, page 9)

The development of the EYP role is to upskill the Early Years workforce and to address the small numbers of graduates working in the private, voluntary and independent sector of Early Years provision. But whether unqualified, graduates or postgraduates, practitioners are expected to be equal members in a children's workforce and have a *'common commitment to improving outcomes for children and young people* (DCSF, 2008a, page 13). To develop *a culture of collaborative and cooperative working* (S33) the expectation is that you will share and discuss ideas and experience together. This can be a challenge. As a prospective EYP, you may have followed a childcare route or graduated in a different discipline and bring transferable skills and experience to your setting. You may, however, come across some cynicism, resentment, or perhaps a lack of co-operation from those who have been working in Early Years settings for a long time and who may not have had the opportunity for training (Miller, 2008). You are likely to have to prove yourself as having something 'extra' to offer as the following case study illustrates.

CASE STUDY

Peggy manages a private nursery. She is a mature woman and began her career as a childminder. Once her children were at school, she took a job at the nursery 'learning on the job' completing her National Vocational Qualification (NVQ) level 3 and NVQ assessors' award and becoming the manager. She takes part in courses and tutors at a local college. Without a degree or adult education trainer qualification, she believes she will no longer be asked to tutor. 'Who are they going to find to do this' she asks 'at the pay we get?' She is sceptical about graduates: 'you first need to see them with the children' she says, 'then you know if they are any good'.

The idea of professionalism is a key component for raising the standards in Early Years and your role as a professional is integral to raising the *status* and *quality* (DfES, 2006a, page 7). As services join together and those who had previously seen their work as mainly with the children extend their work to involve families and the community, professional boundaries are blurring. Who is a 'professional' still resonates negatively in some Early Years settings. It is not easy for some staff, having worked for years in nurseries or playgroups, to accept the EPPE report's findings that state that qualified teachers have the greatest impact on quality in Early Years. This attitude is particularly prevalent where teachers have different working conditions, work for less hours and receive more pay or where they are working with under-threes, a domain that was not previously theirs. A deputy at a children's centre, whose background was not teaching, described a teacher as *frightened to death of going into the baby room*. Nevertheless, she added, the experience had changed the teacher's practice radically, probably more than any other member of staff. The collaboration included learning on both sides. Some practitioners put themselves down, regarding those with qualifications as somehow 'better' than them or, as they frequently put it, 'more educated'. This attitude can create both resentment and nervousness about contributing. Much of it stems from the still-existing perception of Early Years as low-status work.

CASE STUDY

An EYP, also a trained teacher, described her experience:

> *Some of the feelings are historical. Lots of the team have potential, but status and title are important. Some of them still don't believe that they have an impact. They don't see their role as teaching. They are good at putting activities out for the children but if you never say you are a teacher of children you don't have to take responsibility for the children's learning. They assume the teacher is the important person and they used to say to me 'It's your job', which I find frustrating. There has been a change. They are asking why much more now and wanting to discuss what we are doing.*

Defining professionalism

Agreeing a definition of professionalism within Early Years is complicated. Bolam *et al* (2005, page vi) recognise this complexity and suggest that all members of staff, with qualifications or not, are members of professional learning communities. They distinguish between being 'professional' and 'being a professional', highlighting the difference between how people do the job and what qualifications they possess. Their study on effective professional learning communities suggests that the way towards effective professional learning communities depends on adopting *professional standards as the basis for deciding what counts as professional behaviour* and that these standards should be consistent, whatever the nature of the job. Brock (2006) also sees the complex nature of Early Years professionals, where attributes include certain attitudes and values that are not easily assessed, and certainly not through competences. She suggests that if the profession is seeking *the best for children and families* then practitioners *should be expected to be committed, enthusiastic and enjoy their work* (Brock, 2006, page 2). This takes account of the kind of 'professionalism' sought by children and their families. A Scottish survey of parents choosing Early Years provision found that parents' first priority was that their children were happy and safe; secondly, to achieve this, they looked at the quality of care and attitude of staff (Foot *et al*, 2000). In their *Study of Pedagogical Effectiveness in Early Learning* (SPEEL), when parents were asked about the special qualities of practitioners, Moyles *et al* (2002, page 39) found they mainly looked for, what you might call personal rather than professional qualities such as: 'caring attitudes, kindly, sympathetic and loves children'.

A *passion* for the work is an essential attribute, according to Moyles (2001) but it can work against practitioners if they are not able to articulate what they do. Osgood (2006, page 10) argues that *the ethic of care and emotional labour are cornerstones of practitioners' professional identities*, but this kind of professionalism can become denigrated and is not generally valued in the wider society where professionalism is still defined through *masculinised attributes (such as rationality, competitiveness, individualism)* (Osgood, 2006, page 9). She further suggests, citing Novinger and O'Brien (2003), that the government's drive to increase the status of those who work with young children is being carried out by a top-down *technical-rational* model by which practitioners have to demonstrate their competences through 'externally prescribed regulations and standards' (Osgood, 2006, page 9). This does not value the professionalism that includes *high emotion and a culture of care and nurturance.*

Nevertheless, practitioners need to justify and promote their work with children if their status is to increase and they can carry out what they believe is right for children. They will only be able to do this if they are able to reflect on what they are doing and why. Osgood (2006, page 12) believes that an *assertive, self-assured and wise* EYP can *challenge the status quo* and be part of the debate about what it means to be a *professional*. Sam, in the case study below, has worked for 20 years and seen her job change radically as a result of her own learning and ambitions and because of the changing nature of jobs. She represents one of Osgood's EYPs and, as Moss (2008, page 124) describes, is *at home* in an *inclusive, experimenting, creative and democratic early childhood centre.*

CASE STUDY

Sam is deputy head of a nursery school and children's centre. She began as a nursery nurse and has now done the National Professional Qualification in Integrated Centre Leadership (NPQICL). Her passion for her work comes over when she describes what she does and as she says, the qualifications she has attained have, in some ways enhanced this. She feels confident in her role, but perhaps most important, happy to think outside the box. She uses her position to fight tooth and nail for what she believes is right and, with others, can make sure things on offer benefit the children. She is developing her own role as she works across services. Demanding good practice, she is prepared to argue for resources and, having always developed good relationships with others outside, makes demands on them, placing the child at the centre of her actions. For example, she felt perfectly justified in insisting that a social worker, who had wanted a mother and child to come to her office, came to meet them at the centre because there was a possibility that the child was to be taken into care. Sam argued that the child needed to be in an environment where he felt secure, not in an unfamiliar office.

REFLECTIVE TASK

How would you describe yourself as a professional? What is it that makes you feel professional?

What attributes of professionalism would you look for when colleagues are interacting with:

- *children;*
- *parents and carers;*
- *other colleagues?*

The SPEEL report (Moyles *et al*, 2002, page 8) describes effective Early Years practitioners as *'possess*[ing] *and apply*[ing] *to their practices specific values, qualities, knowledge and thinking which ensure they have a positive effect on children's learning and development*. The report highlighted how many practitioners could describe the practical provision they made for children but not articulate the rationale of their actions and how it impacted on the children. Once practitioners recognise and value what they have to offer then they can build on this. The first steps to becoming *professional* are *a positive disposition to learn* and being *capable of extending* [oneself] *professionally* (Moyles *et al*, 2002, page 5). You will need to consider environments that encourage practitioners to learn and think professionally (S38, S39). Some practitioners in your team may have had bad learning experiences in the past. They may find it hard to risk giving their opinion in case it is 'wrong'. You can play a big role in challenging a concept of professionalism that is linked to status, encouraging others to develop their skills and knowledge through discussions within the team and further training. Just as children learn through talking about what they are doing so practitioners too need opportunities to *articulate and evaluate* (Moyles *et al*, 2002, page 5) their practice.

Training for professionals

Recent training initiatives for the Early Years workforce which emphasise competence rather than discourse may on the surface raise standards but Moss, (2008, page 123) cautions that there is a danger that practitioners become *technicians trained in right answers* and that they *consume knowledge rather than construct* it with children and other adults (Rinaldi, 2006, page 135). It is possible for practitioners to mark a checklist to see if a child is capable of using scissors but they also need to understand the child's potential and their own role in developing this. This comes through an *intuitive intelligence*, developed through systematic reflection and experience with many children and in many different environments (Laevers, 2005).

With the need to look at the broad outcomes of the Childcare Act (2006) that highlight the social needs of children as well as the curriculum and the idea of a universal service, practitioners have had to respond to a different way of working. Research carried out internationally supports the idea that *investment in professional ECEC* (Early Childhood Education and Care) *staff is a preferable strategy for raising quality than over prescribing a centralized curriculum* (Bertram and Pascal, 2002, page ii). Professional learning is sometimes equated with individual professional development where people go on a course or learn strategies for working with children, say, with behaviour or language difficulties. There is obviously a place for this individual expertise but developing a joint knowledge base will require looking together at how you work with the children. Siraj-Blatchford and Manni (2006, page 19) found that effective settings had an *informal-formal* approach to staff development. There were observations and discussion with practitioners on an informal day-to-day basis but this was combined with more formal meetings where staff reflected on their work and received individual feedback. MacNaughton (2005, page 201) stresses the *transformative* nature of learning as a group. With *encouragement and inspiration* you can *plunge into new ways of thinking and acting*. She cites Foucault's (1983) distinction between the *will to know* and the *will to truth*, suggesting that the facts, for instance about child development, are subjective and that there are multiple views and contradictions. Moving from the will to know to the will to truth can be risky as it may go against received wisdom or the status quo but it moves us on in our knowledge.

The *quick fix* emphasises techniques and methods (MacNaughton, 2005). The kind of dilemmas practitioners come across are *paradoxical* (Moyles, 2001); they do not have simple answers. MacNaughton (2005) suggests that the impact of one-off workshops is minimal: only 16–20% of participants will have taken up the recommendations and those who do put them into practice could have learnt these by reading a book. Since practitioners often want a straightforward answer, particularly when they are having difficulties, it is easy to come up with a pat one. But when set strategies do not work practitioners can feel confused or guilty (MacNaughton, 2005).

REFLECTIVE TASK

- *Do you think there is a place for set strategies? If so, what and when?*

- *Do you agree that set strategies can leave practitioners feeling 'confused' and 'guilty' when they do not work?*

Developing professional thinking in a team

Professional educare (Anning and Edwards, 2006) demands new ways of thinking and different contexts for working together. These contexts need to be *safe and well-supported* as practitioners are asked to discuss their practice with others and possibly change the way they do things. Professional communities, like teams, evolve and are on a continuum; they mature (Bolam *et al*, 2005) as practitioners develop their professional thinking. Oberheumer's (2005) model of *democratic professionalism*, which you considered in terms of leadership in Chapter 3, encourages practitioners to interact with children, developing listening skills so they are involved in *shared thinking* (Siraj-Blatchford *et al*, 2002) and children become part of *democratic dialogue and decision-making* (Oberheumer, 2005, page 13). This participatory culture with children is reflected in the way practitioners share tasks and specialist knowledge. In actively seeking others' knowledge and expertise, there is an acceptance that there are *multiple ways of knowing*. Democratic professionalism demands practitioners to reflect on their *taken-for-granted beliefs* to become *intellectually curious* (Rinaldi, 2006, page 135). It requires they look at their practice differently and question whether it is the best way. This can be uncomfortable, particularly for those who have done little formal learning, and possibly none since school. Moving from the type of learning that answers the question *Am I doing it right?* to a reflective approach where there are *multiple ways of knowing* is exciting, but quite scary for the less confident.

As the demands on practitioners to think more critically about their practice increase, they will need to *feel comfortable to open up and share thoughts in an environment where there is no right answer* (MacNaughton, 2005, page 198). As the EYP, your role will be to encourage practitioners to look deeper into their practice, and develop a broader knowledge and experience about the children they work with and the environment they live in.

CASE STUDY

Sally, introduced in Chapter 2, qualified as a nursery nurse 20 years ago and, having brought up her own children and worked for 17 years in the same nursery, believed that what she had learnt was the right way of working. Nevertheless, when the county offered funding to undertake a foundation degree, she decided to take the opportunity. She found herself totally enthused. She looked at the theory behind the practice, and began asking questions and looking at things in different ways. She noticed the space outside; the nursery was surrounded by fields with a pond nearby and she had never fully recognised its potential. She realised she could take the 'inside' out and transformed it, and the children 'camped' outside for three weeks. She began to convince her colleagues that it was worth doing things differently. She said 'I have to chip away slowly sometimes with my new ideas but now the rest of them come along and say "I'm not sure about this, but shall we try it?"'

Practitioners may need assistance in recognising their contribution in creating a sustainable joint knowledge base from which to work and develop. But as Anning and Edwards (2006) suggest, *the adults' love of learning will have a direct effect on children's appetite to learn*. The difference between a professional development and skills approach means reflecting on 'why' we offer children particular learning opportunities as much as 'how' we do this. Hay (2008, page 100) recognises that it is hard to give time to purposeful reflection with the pressures to *satisfy regulators, parents and employers*, and it is easy to get caught up in the day-to-day activities. But, as she suggests, *purposeful reflection* is essential for better outcomes for children, and working together allows you to be open to new ways of thinking and to take risks. MacNaughton (2005) gives examples from a project where practitioners had opportunities to reflect on their work, their enthusiasm for doing this and the need for building this into the practice. When asked what critical reflection meant, one practitioner saw it as *not talking about mundane issues that I solve day to day but major issues* (MacNaughton, 2005, page 195). Another, who often came back fired up from one-off training days, found that unless these were followed up, her enthusiasm faded:

> Motivation is a big factor – me, I'm like a little seed in the ground, in a hole in a rut waiting to bloom. I don't want to be a wilted seed in the garden! Like a gerbera that stands up and then goes eeeeeer . . .

> (MacNaughton, 2005, page 190)

Like Hay (2008), MacNaughton (2005) recognises follow up involves an investment in time and a change in the way practitioners think about their work; she argues for a change in focus in professional learning with opportunities to discuss *big ideas* (MacNaughton, 2005, page 197).

Researchers and policy makers continually advocate the need for practitioners to meet together and find time to reflect on their work. But as more and more parents demand childcare, restructuring to reduce the workload for individual practitioners is a tall order. The policy makers and decision makers have a key role in this too in, *match*[ing] *current rhetoric about the need for collaboration with resources in the form of staff training and time* [my emphasis] *to make this possible* (Darlington *et al*, 2005, page 246). Children centres' leaders have the will and see the need to work with others but the question of time comes up continually (Needham, 2008). Yet time can become an excuse not to do anything. *'Collaborative inertia'* (DfES, 2007b) may set in when people become over-whelmed by what has to be done.

REFLECTIVE TASK

- *Do you agree with the practitioner above that the mundane day-to-day issues get in the way of looking at some of the major issues of working with young children?*

- *How do you see your role in encouraging practitioners to create space and opportunities to explore some 'big ideas'?*

Communities of practice

The experience of learning for many practitioners, and this may include you, has been something that you do on your own (Stoll, 2004). The idea of learning as a community suggests working together with common goals and shared beliefs.

Lave and Wenger (1991) introduced the concept of *communities of practice*. In the same way as children learn in social and cultural contexts (Vygotsky, 1978; Rogoff, 1990), adults too learn through participation and collaboration with others. Communities of practice are everywhere; we learn at work, at home and in our leisure time. They can be quite fluid, others more organized, but their main purpose is to share ideas and negotiate meaning. They are more than a discussion group, however, being a place to embrace new ideas and learn from what others bring. Siraj-Blatchford and Manni (2006, page 18) cite Biggs' concept (1996, page 6) that reflective practice is not just a mirror that reflects back the image. Through critical analysis, it reveals other dimensions, initially hidden, to show *what it might be, an improvement on the original*. This in turn motivates and encourages ongoing learning and development.

In their research, Bolam *et al* (2005, page iii) defined effective learning communities as having: *the capacity to promote and sustain the learning of all professionals in the* [school] *community with the collective purpose of enhancing pupil learning*. Wenger (1998) emphasises that although members of communities of practice have different roles, they have complementary contributions to make. Therefore . . . *it is more important to know how to give and receive help than to try to know everything yourself* (Wenger, 1998, page 76). This is a good starting point for you when you are developing your work with other adults and children. Wenger identifies two processes that complement each other: participation and reification. *Participation* involves sharing genuine experiences and interactions so members can work towards a common goal (Anning, 2001). Thus, practitioners will discuss their ongoing experiences working with children and parents and share their expertise. *Reification* goes deeper and involves making abstract ideas concrete. For example how do you envisage children's play outside? What is your expectation of parents' role within the setting?

Anning (2001) distinguishes between the conceptual and experiential knowledge bases: conceptual knowledge, relevant to the work, is learnt through training; experiential knowledge is based on the experience of what happens. She suggests that because experiential knowledge is based on the daily routines, it is often unspoken knowledge. Thus, when staff have been working together for a long time, this knowledge is taken for granted and new members of staff, especially less experienced ones, may take the current way of doing things as a given. When practitioners from different services work together, many of these practices are suddenly open to scrutiny. There may be a common goal, *children's welfare*, but differences of opinion can arise in the way this is translated into practice and how practitioners' roles are redefined or reassigned. We look further at this in Chapter 8. It is through bringing these differences into the open, however, that members of the group acquire new forms of knowledge, relevant to the new way of working (Anning, 2001). If these differences are not confronted and discussed, then there is no possibility of moving on or improving the practice. As practitioners with different experiences join together in teams, there are two challenges; the first is to create new professional identities (who I am); the second, to *articulate and share their personal and professional knowledge in order to create new versions of knowledge (what I know) for new ways of working* (Anning, 2001, page 9).

REFLECTIVE TASK

- *How, if at all, has your professional identity changed in the last five years or, is changing in the work you do now?*

- *What new knowledge have you had to gain, or need to explore, in order to work in a different way?*

Developing shared values and vision in a learning community

Bolam et al (2005, page i) identified the following key features in a professional learning community:

- *shared values and vision;*
- *collective responsibility for children's learning;*
- *collaboration focused on learning;*
- *individual and collective professional learning;*

- *reflective professional enquiry;*

- *openness, networks and partnerships;*

- *inclusive membership.*

To create this, they suggested, members needed to develop *mutual trust, respect and support*. We considered in Chapter 2 the importance of a team having a shared vision with common underlying values. Personal value systems can influence professional thinking and development (Rodd, 2006, page 111). Unless staff acknowledge and discuss their beliefs and share their differences, the messages children and their families may receive could be ambiguous. As the following case study illustrates, the professional beliefs may not accord with personal beliefs.

CASE STUDY

Marianne expressed her dilemma in having personal and professional values that are at odds. Personally she believes in very young children being at home for the first few years; she was able to stay at home with hers. She worries about mothers being encouraged to return to work as soon as possible. Professionally she understands that the centre she works at is offering a service for parents who want or need to work for all sorts of reasons. She recognises that she has a choice about working in such an environment and cannot let her personal values get in the way. The children don't have a choice. Thus, although holding a personal belief, as a professional she believes that the children and parents deserve the best.

REFLECTIVE TASK

- *Are you aware of any of your personal values clashing with the professional ones?*

- *How do you reconcile these?*

Although you may have guidelines for acceptable practice, it is difficult to impose values. Rinaldi (2006, page 165) describes the impossibility of *selling the Reggio method* that cannot be transported because of its cultural context. Underlying this 'method' are ethical values, brought about through reflection and discussion with an underpinning belief in the competent child. Anning and Edwards (2006), in their work as researchers with practitioners, emphasise the importance of going slowly, building relationships and sharing concerns. As you will see in the next chapter, prior to a shared understanding, you may experience conflict and uncertainty. Practitioners may carry out the practice competently but it is only when there is a real belief in what they are doing that they can feel a sense of achievement and fulfilment. When you are new, developing new ways of working or supporting staff with little experience, it is easy to focus on what has to be done or achieved next. Shared values do not arrive overnight and it can be frustrating to have to return again and again to discussions about attitudes.

Carrying out the key principles within the stated vision of your work will be affected by the underlying values. Vision statements often appear fairly straightforward but may have taken a long time to come about. Stirling Children's Partnership in Scotland has worked together and come up with four main underpinning principles to their practice:

- putting children first;

- inclusion;

- quality;

- partnership.

(Kinney, 2005, page 112)

As principles, you might expect everyone to agree with these. But discussion amongst a team can reveal differences in interpretation or, as discussed in Chapter 2, a *false clarity*. Underneath these statements are big agendas that need to be understood and acknowledged. What does it mean to put children first? Do you put children at the centre of the decisions you make? Are children listened to?

REFLECTIVE TASK

Below is a 'vision statement' from a children's centre that is typical of many others:

> *Our Children's Centre is committed to enhancing Early Years education and childcare provision. We aim to provide high quality affordable childcare for all children.*

> *In addition, we aim to provide a focal point in the local community to meet and respond to the growing needs of families. We will offer families access to health and educational training courses with a view to improving their employment prospects.*

> *The Children's Centre offers a safe, secure and fun environment where children and parents can develop and achieve their full potential. We aim to make a positive contribution to the community by working in partnership with parents and professionals.*

Having read this statement, consider:

- *What are the underpinning principles in this statement?*

- *What would this vision look like in practice – i.e. enhancing Early Years education?*

- *Consider the principles that underpin your own practice.*

- *If you have a vision statement, look at it and see whether these principles would be evident to a reader?*

Collective responsibility and collaboration for children's learning

The government's expectation is that the introduction of the EYFS will raise educational standards throughout all settings. Putting this into practice has required some settings to rethink the way they work with children, to be much more accountable and to understand the relationship between education and care. Eyles (2007) describes an Early Years mentor teacher scheme, where teachers worked in different Early Years settings to raise quality and standards. This had to be done sensitively and she stresses the collaborative nature of the work. Although the mentors were asked to support others in developing quality provision, it was because they took on a facilitative role and acknowledged others' expertise and experience – finding common ground from which to move forwards – that they began to disseminate good practice. Developing empathetic relationships and sharing professional expertise while focusing on the children's learning was an integral part of the project's success. Collaborating in this way allowed those working together to feel they had a vital part to play and to share ownership. The professional rapport that was built up increased opportunities to collaborate; this in turn was *influential in supporting and improving quality practices* (Eyles, 2007, page 134). The mentors were enthusiastic and gained confidence working outside their usual setting. They also began to recognise the gaps within their own knowledge because of the diverse settings, and needed support to develop their knowledge and reflect on their own practice and expertise. For any support programme to impact on the quality of work, Eyles (2007, page 136) suggests, there needs to be *a shared philosophy* that must *focus on children and maintain*[ing] *high quality early years learning and care environments* and this requires a professional understanding. A shared professional understanding may take time to develop but you can make a difference if you encourage dialogue and exploration. As Moyles (2001, page 89) suggests: *Educational improvement depends upon practitioners feeling they WANT to make a difference: upon them feeling empowered and professional.*

C H A P T E R   S U M M A R Y

This chapter has looked at the complexities of developing a sense of equality in teams where there may be a great range of qualifications. We have looked at your role as a 'professional' and at some of the arguments around what professionalism means in Early Years. We have asked you to think about your role in developing learning communities where practitioners can discuss and reflect on their own and others' practice and realise that there are no simple answers.

Moving on

The next chapter considers the challenges for practitioners in managing change. It looks at the different types of change they may experience and your role in managing it yourself and supporting others through it. It considers how conflict may arise because of changing circumstances but sees it as a natural part of the working environment. It suggests ways for EYPs to challenge and confront others and to give critical feedback assertively.

Self-assessment exercise

In their analysis of collaboration within the team, the SPEEL research team identified a range of factors for success. Using the following headings taken from their analysis (Moyles *et al*, 2002, page 30) reflect on your team and, using the table below, note down some examples of ways you and your colleagues can develop collaborative practice.

Supporting effective teamwork through:	My role	The role of other members of the team
Communication		
Involving practitioners		
Sharing practice		
Establishing a shared sense of purpose		
Developing good relationships with adults and children		
Demonstrating collaboration to other adults and children		

FURTHER READING

Eyles, J (2007) Vision, mission, method: challenges and issues in developing the role of the early years mentor teacher, Chapter 8, in Moyles, J (ed) (2007) *Early years foundations: meeting the challenge*. Maidenhead: Open University Press.

Moss, P (2008) The democratic and reflective professional: rethinking and reforming the early years workforce, Chapter 11, in Miller, L, Cable, C (eds) *Professionalism in the early years*. Abingdon: Hodder Education.

Wenger, E (1998) *Communities of practice: a brief introduction*. Cambridge: Cambridge University Press.

www.ewenger.com/theory/

7 Managing change

Introduction

Who are you? said the Caterpillar . . . Alice replied, rather shyly, I – I hardly know, sir, just at present – at least I knew who I was when I got up this morning, but I think I must have changed several times since then.

(Lewis Caroll, 1865)

Those who have worked in Early Years during the last few years will probably recognise Alice's feelings. The government's different strategies to reshape and reform services for children and their families have brought profound changes for practitioners in the settings they work in and their practice. New government legislation or restructuring of services can overwhelm practitioners with fear, resentment or just sheer hard work, so that it detracts from the good practice that has always existed. McCullough (2007) points out that although the changes in *Every Child Matters* and the Children Act, 2004 have been called *innovative and challenging*, in the case of child protection work, social workers already had an established practice based on sound principles that included collaboration. The *problem lay in the inconsistency of implementation*, McCullough argues, not in the underlying principles (McCullough, 2007, page 43). Seeing change then as a process and a way of developing the work that has gone before, rather than as a distinctive event, eases much of the anxiety.

Change as a process

Any dynamic and living organisation will be changing every day. Changing the way you do things is stimulating as long as you experience some stability. As one outreach worker commented *I never know what I'm going to find. Every day is different. That's why I love the work . . . But*, she reflected: *there are days when I am not sure what I have done, especially when I've worked with someone who's finding life very difficult*. We referred to the *rigorous and challenging* team in Chapter 2 (Edgington, 2004, page 54) and considered the importance of stopping from time to time to look at what it has achieved. Change can come slowly or sometimes almost imperceptibly, and often practitioners are so busy they do not have time to reflect on the changes they have made either to their own practice or to families' lives. Part of your role as an EYP is to encourage staff to implement new ways of working with the children but also to reflect on how they are building on existing practice to improve what they offer.

CASE STUDY

During a discussion about their vision for a newly formed children's centre, a group of senior managers – including an EYP – reflected on its changing aspects. Working with other agencies presented them with challenges about where their individual roles and responsibilities in the children's centre began and ended. Having a greater understanding of the community outside the nursery had impacted on their knowledge. They were, they felt, working within a fragmented community over which they had little control. What opportunities were there for children to continue the experience they had at the children's centre once they left? How was childhood valued outside? They had to think globally as well as locally. They recognised that thinking globally could be overwhelming yet their contribution locally must not be devalued.

They concluded that other staff, especially those working mainly with the children, did not necessarily recognise their contribution within the broader context. Staff were very involved in helping children to achieve and enjoy. They were also providing contexts, such as outings and social events, where parents could relax and enjoy their children and, in their daily interactions with them, shared their thoughts and information about the children. The managers decided it was important to organise a training day, not on learning some new skill or looking at a new initiative but to reflect on the staff's contribution to a service that had changed for them but where the principles remained the same.

The challenges of change

The role of the EYP is to be a *catalyst for change and innovation* (CWDC, 2008a, page 5). This can be a challenge however if you find yourself caught in the middle, putting up with the moans or anxieties of your immediate colleagues, particularly when the idea for changing has come from elsewhere. Practitioners may be committed to a more cohesive service for families but the reality of working in this way demands huge changes professionally and psychologically. Duffy and Marshall (2007, page 110) point out that there is frequently nostalgia for the past and it takes sensitivity, creativity and an enthusiastic approach to help teams move on and accept the changes. Even when the old ways were not particularly good, some may find it easier to cling to the old ways or look back to 'a golden age'. Genuine change takes time and is an evolving process. Talk to Early Years practitioners who have been working for some years and you will find they have often forgotten the huge anxieties they felt previously as they took on new challenges. For example, a group of practitioners were extremely worried about how they would cope, and quite resistant to the idea, when a nursery school and a centre for children with multiple disabilities were combined as a children's centre several years ago. Staff now find it hard to recognise their deep anxieties at that time and see inclusion as a natural part of their work. They have extended their ways of thinking, developed relationships with children and colleagues, and taken on new roles and responsibilities. The children's centre has undergone massive structural change, as the building was re-modelled, but there is now a team of enthusiastic and committed practitioners.

Types of change

Rodd (2006, page 185) identifies the different levels of change that occur, which range from the everyday, *incremental* change, through planning meetings or general day-to-day discussions, to *transformational* change where the organisation is radically altered. Routine change is common and includes changes to shift patterns, activities and timetable. Consistent systems will help practitioners to manage these. But as services join up and children centres expand across the country, many Early Years practitioners will be undergoing or have undergone transformational change.

As an EYP, you are most likely to be involved in innovative and induced change (Whalley, 2008). Induced change occurs when individuals or the team recognise that a system or a structure is not working and needs altering either completely or partially. This could be as a result of a crisis or, as is common, a routine matter (Rodd, 2006). Innovative change, usually the result of creative thinking, generally takes place, suggests Rodd (2006), when a team is working co-operatively and collaboratively together or a leader wants to bring in new ideas to develop the way you work. A mature team will respond to the needs of the children and families and will be ready to try out new ideas and want to be creative in their work. This type of change requires flexibility and may mean taking risks and, to be effective, demands a real commitment to carry through the process with constant monitoring formally or informally. As Rodd (2006) suggests, there needs to be a fundamental raison d'être for innovative change if it is to be successful, so that it does not just become change for change's sake. When practitioners are involved in both innovative and induced change, even if it is introduced as a result of a crisis, they manage it more successfully than when they feel it is imposed.

CASE STUDY

Fran, a local authority development worker, supports pre-schools, childminders and private nurseries. Some of the practitioners in these settings are struggling with putting the EYFS into practice. They believe that what they have been offering is what parents and children want and that the EYFS is just another time-consuming imposition. There were two areas Fran had to tackle; the first was to reassure the practitioners that their practice was not necessarily 'bad' and that it was possible to build on what they were doing already. She has had to establish relationships with them so they don't feel she is the 'expert' coming in to tell them what to do. The second was to break down the areas of the EYFS for them so that they were not overwhelmed by the documentation. She then suggested and discussed practical activities that they could carry out.

PRACTICAL TASK

1 *Choose one of the six areas covered by the early learning goals and educational programmes in the EYFS Statutory Framework (DCSF, 2008b):*

- *personal, social and emotional development;*
- *communication, language and literacy;*
- *problem solving, reasoning and numeracy;*
- *knowledge and understanding of the world;*
- *physical development;*
- *creative development.*

2 *Reflect on Fran's experience in the case study above.*

3 *Then consider how you would introduce this area, and the early learning goals that correspond, with another practitioner or group of practitioners in putting a programme into practice:*

a *they reflect on their previous practice and see the strengths within this;*

b *they begin to reflect on ways they can build on what they already know;*

c *they develop some further strategies for developing their practice.*

4 *How would you follow up the work you do with them?*

There is often resentment when people believe they are 'having things done to them'. Fran recognised this attitude in some practitioners. She had to balance supporting them in their anxiety and improving the practice. She realised that if she did not listen to their concerns and frustrations that they would carry out the activities with the children when she was there but not do them otherwise. She had to listen to and acknowledge their concerns but not allow these to dominate discussions. She also had to present her ideas in a way that would not negate what they had been doing already.

Your role in managing change

We all experience change in our lives, and understanding your own ability to manage this will give you insights into how others may feel. Some practitioners who fear change may have stayed in the same role for years, losing confidence about their potential. They begin to feel de-skilled, and do not recognise their transferable skills and experience. A series of changes coming together can easily take away people's confidence and self-esteem. Sudden change can shock people into inactivity. They need hope and the possibility that there will be some benefits. Most changes in Early Years are not unexpected. In fact, a great problem is that practitioners know that there will be changes but are not clear about what these will be, as discussions around legislation take place or local authorities decide to reorganise. The worst stage for people is when they don't know what is going to happen and cannot envisage the future. They cannot see it in practical terms. It is in this period that rumours begin to abound and a team can drift into a spiral of gloom. Once you know what will change, then, even if you do not like it, you can begin to accept it and take action to manage it.

Change brings gains and losses. Losses are not always negative or straightforward and can bring gains with them: for example, a practitioner, although sad to lose her small, intimate team, found it much more exhilarating working with a range of practitioners. But to move through change, people need accurate information and opportunities to talk and ask questions, and the more involved they are, the more they are able to accept it. We talk a great deal about the importance of praise and reassurance for children, but it is easy to forget that adults need this too. We manage change in different ways. You will remember Belbin's different role types within a team, discussed in Chapter 2. Some people like an ordered life with routines and the future planned; others are spontaneous, living in the present and ready to plan at the last minute and see what happens. Neither is necessarily better, but these individuals are likely to cope with change in different ways. When you are responsible for bringing in changes, you may sometimes have to introduce them slowly; at other times, speed will lessen practitioners' anxieties so they do not constantly worry about what has not yet happened.

Maggie, as a newly arrived EYP, explained some of the ways she tried to change the practice in her room:

> *I've never been shy about saying things because I feel confident about what I do. But I have discovered that you have to discuss things, bring people with you. I don't expect everything to change immediately and I am biding my time but I feel people trust me more and I can feel the time is coming when I can ask for more. The question I ask them when we are discussing issues is: how do you think that affects the children? They are more likely to see the reason for changing things if I put it that way than saying this is what we're going to do.*

Maggie was aware that she could not ask for too much at a time and she was not expecting the change to happen immediately. But she also recognised that the team was working through a process and coming to a point where they would be willing and confident to try out some new ways.

Even when change is positive, it can be challenging to manage. Taking on new responsibilities can be exciting but also demanding. Recognising what you can and cannot change or influence helps you to focus on what is realistic. It is easy to expend a huge amount of energy on something you cannot change. For example, you cannot usually completely change the physical nature of your setting. You may well have to 'live' with certain inconvenient spaces or danger spots. The energy needs to go on making the most of these rather than bemoaning the fact that they are not ideal, something that some practitioners are prone to do and which it is easy to get caught up in. There has to be a balance between people expressing their concerns and actually getting on with what has to be done. You can help by directing people to seeing what they can change for themselves and what they can change with help.

The *Every Child Matters* guidance for managing change cites the following as the most common challenges managers have to take on when developing multi-agency teams:

- helping people perceive their role in terms of outcomes rather than their professional backgrounds;

- helping practitioners re-interpret their professional role against a backdrop of changed expectations about how professionals should operate in a group;

- managing the anxiety of professionals who may be anxious that parts of their job can be done by staff who do not share their qualifications;

- managing the anxiety of unqualified support workers that their skills are ignored by professionally qualified colleagues;

- positioning the team so it can act as a catalyst for systemic change where necessary;

- overcoming cultural and practice barriers to achieve common goals and maximum productivity;

- a reluctance to 'step out of the box' and work in new and flexible ways to support children, young people and families (**www.everychildmatters.gov.uk/delivering services/multiagencyworking/managerstoolkit/managingchange/**).

REFLECTIVE TASK

We have looked at some of these issues in previous chapters. Having read the challenges above:

- *Can you recognise any of them as relating to yourself?*

- *What do you think are the main challenges for the other staff with whom you work?*

- *How do you think the team can support each other in facing these challenges?*

Why conflict?

Inevitably, however well you get on with your team and colleagues, you will have to face situations that are difficult and deal with conflicting ideas and practice. Conflict is often regarded as negative or a failure and denied or hidden in Early Years settings. Rodd (2006, page 105) sees Early Years contexts as *ripe arenas* for conflict as there are many different philosophies and views, derived from personal experience, about the best ways of caring for and educating children. The subjectivity of these views can lead to personal disputes between practitioners and with parents. A dynamic and developing team will inevitably come up against differences amongst members and with others outside. There is also potential conflict when different services join together and practitioners begin to express differing viewpoints. Chandler (2006, quoted in DfES, 2007a) suggests that there are three areas that influence practitioners' contribution to multi-agency work: their personal history and reasons for choosing the work; previous experience and training; and the beliefs, values, and aims and objectives for the service in which they work. Reading the literature on Early Years you can also see that there are many different perspectives. These differences may manifest themselves as disputes but can nonetheless result in creative and new ways of thinking and doing things. Conflict does not necessarily mean that practitioners do not agree about the goals they want to achieve but rather that they disagree about the way they do this.

Understanding where and why the conflict has arisen means that you can take steps to either resolve it or use appropriate strategies to manage it. In Chapter 3 you looked at the importance of the structure and systems, and these can have an enormous effect on whether things go smoothly or not. For example, lack of opportunities to meet or staff shortages can easily result in misunderstandings and arguments.

REFLECTIVE TASK

- *Think about some of the factors present in organisations that lead to conflict.*

- *Think about some of the personal factors that lead to conflict.*

Passion for the work (Moyles, 2001) and Early Years practitioners' reliance on goodwill forestalls much of the potential conflict built into the organisation. Nevertheless there are some areas – such as terms and conditions of employment – that are inbuilt areas to watch. The CWDC is developing an Integrated Qualifications Framework (IQF) so that all practitioners can progress across the children's workforce, but currently hours of work and pay still differ enormously. The integration of Early Years services encourages practitioners to take on more responsibility. However, it requires a fine judgment to recognise the difference between exploitation and giving responsibility when practitioners love their work and contribute willingly to the team.

Lack of resources or a sense that some areas do better than others can lead to demotivation or general moaning. Practitioners speak of the times when they are under pressure or the team is tired as dangerous moments for clashes or misunderstandings. Lack of leadership or decision making can also lead to people feeling undervalued or frustrated. Changing the structure of services can bring a loss of professional identity (French, 2007) and confusion about responsibilities. You read earlier about childminders who can feel that their autonomy is being eroded. As services begin to work more closely together, there are often historical barriers and stereotypes that may need breaking down. Multiprofessional teams coming from a range of social, cultural and professional backgrounds may have different ways of interpreting policy and practice. In some circumstances, practitioners are expected to come to decisions about support for families with others they may hardly know. Sometimes these relationships are virtual and developed telephonically or electronically. Some teams can feel they are being taken over or dominated by larger or more high-profile ones. With greater resources, large children's centres, representing the 'hub' can be threatening for those who remain the 'spokes' as parents choose the more high-profile settings in the neighbourhood or the one that can offer more hours. Expectations change too. As Bertram *et al* (2002, page 53) suggest, there can be a tension when 'child-centred' and 'parent-centred' goals are in competition.

CASE STUDY

Rachel, an outreach worker, had a serious fall-out with a practitioner working in the children's room. They were both committed to good practice and held similar values about what they were offering. But it was their views on working with parents that differed. Rachel saw her priority as supporting the parent, visiting her regularly and encouraging her to come to the groups at the children's centre and to sign up for vocational training. Louise felt that Rachel was spending too much time with the mother and not focusing enough on the child who was attending very irregularly.

Managing conflict

Some teams, as you considered earlier, avoid conflict and either deny its existence or shy away from it. The difficulty with this is that the resentment or irritations can increase and then become a huge issue, creating blocks so it is difficult to move on to discuss differences. This may well end in a huge explosion with all the consequences this brings with it. Since many of us fear conflict, we try to suppress it or smooth it over. Of course, there may be times when this is the right strategy particularly if it is a minor irritation or can be dealt with quickly. The first signs of conflict may, however, be the tip of an iceberg and hide something deeper. You need to know what is creating the irritation and whether it is something that can be changed or may have to be lived with. You may want to smooth it over because you want to retain good relations yourself or between others. Nonetheless, confronting and challenging issues can be extremely helpful to everyone, leading to a better understanding. Confronting does not necessarily have to mean a battle, but involves creating an environment, as discussed in Chapter 5, where people talk openly and honestly without seeing differences as a personal attack. You can help by allowing others to express their opinions and listening to these respectfully but also being clear about what you believe.

Facing criticism

It is likely you will be on the receiving end of criticism. When the criticism comes as a shock it is particularly difficult to manage. But being able to manage this assertively will help you when you have to give 'critical' feedback to others.

CASE STUDY

Lisa recalls her experience at a multi-agency meeting:

> *We were discussing services in the neighbourhood and there seemed to be a general feeling that we were working well together. Suddenly, one of the members looked at me and said that our admissions policy had meant that a parent had been excluded. I was shocked because I know we are very careful about this. I sat there not knowing what to say. Then I started justifying myself and completely went off the point. I felt I had let myself down and everyone at our centre.*

Like Lisa, people often hear criticism as a reflection on them personally rather than about their performance in the job (Back and Back, 2005) since their experience of 'critical' feedback has frequently been negative. One definition of *critical* in the Collins dictionary is *containing analytical evaluation*, and you can also see it as a *critical point*, a time when something needs to change. In a group asked to give personal examples of receiving critical feedback, only one could identify a situation where they had felt comfortable and found it useful. Being able to give helpful critical feedback is, however, an important skill if you want to make changes. Much of our reluctance or anxiety about listening to feedback comes from our past experience when criticism has been unhelpful and not accurate. Memories of childhood labels can skew the way you hear what others say. For example, when someone suggests you could do something in a different way, you may inwardly hear a parent, teacher or sibling saying *there you go, doing it wrong again*. You defend yourself, often in the way you did in the past with a counter-attack, blaming others or yourself. Either way, you begin to cut off from what is being said.

The main way to handle criticism assertively is to listen carefully. This can be hard to do because when criticism comes as a personal attack, it often resonates in such a way that it is difficult to recognise what is actually being said. If the criticism is untrue, then it is best to say so briefly. You are hearing another's opinion; this is not necessarily a fact. You may want to explain why you believe it is untrue but you do not want to get into the kind of *oh yes it is, oh no it isn't argument* that does not help the communication. When criticism comes as a personal attack, it is easy to defend or attack back but it could be something outside your control and you need to know more. This is the time to pause, think and take a deep breath before replying.

In Lisa's case, there was some truth in the allegation. A parent had not been offered a place at the centre. However, the admissions policy was fair and she had not been 'excluded'. Lisa had seen this word as pejorative and focused on it. She needed to respond to the criticism itself, asking further questions. She might start by 'fielding' the remark by acknowledging the parent did not get a place but asking for more information: *why do you say this? What makes you believe she was excluded?* This opens up the communication. Asking for more information, when it is a personal attack on you with no justification, means the other person has to think about what he or she said. Of course, there will be times when the criticism is true. This is not necessarily easy to accept, but admitting your mistake is more respectful than pretending it did not happen. When critical feedback is offered respectfully, it can be helpful and an opportunity to change or learn something new. Whether you hear it accurately or not will depend on the way it is given.

Giving critical feedback to others

As an EYP you have to *ensure that colleagues . . . understand their role and are involved appropriately in helping children to meet planned objectives* (S34). You will have to give feedback and ask them to do things differently. Some practitioners may deny their weaknesses but, equally, others may deny their strengths. Challenge from another practitioner who believes you could be achieving more can be stimulating and motivating. Helping someone to see that the way they see a situation or themselves in it does not match how you or others see it, can be helpful and enlightening if done sensitively.

CASE STUDY

Profile books are an important resource in the setting where Firdousie works and there had been much discussion about how to use these with children and adults so they gave a picture of each child. Lili found them a challenge and complained that they took up too much time. Firdousie knew that she had to talk to Lili about her observations. Finding it hard to receive criticism herself, Firdousie was tentative about raising the subject, thinking that Lili would see it as an attack on her personally. Lili was a very good practitioner but had little confidence in her abilities, particularly her writing skills. Firdousie wanted to convince her that these were valuable records for the children and adults and at the same time help her to write in a more focused way.

She had a choice; to leave it and hope Lili would just improve by seeing how others wrote; or to give her some direction. Her ideal scenario was that Lili improved anyway. Being idealistic can be positive but in this case it was not realistic. Firdousie needed to change the situation now. She recognised she had responsibility to improve practice and also the right to ask. She wanted to raise the quality of the profile books and to support Lili's professional development.

REFLECTIVE TASK

What suggestions would you give to Firdousie so that Lili hears this feedback as helpful rather than as criticism of her abilities?

Ignoring a situation or waiting for something to go wrong again means that when you do eventually give feedback you are often irritated or frustrated and can easily become aggressive. On the receiving end, aggressive behaviour can make you feel like a child being told off. Where and when you receive the feedback will also make a difference to how you hear it.

CASE STUDY *continued*

Firdousie decided to meet Lili in a small room, familiar to both of them and private. It is important to think about the place because some practitioners express their nervousness or resentment when they are called to the 'office' with its connotations of being in trouble at school. Preparing what you want to say means that you can give concrete feedback, based on observation. Firdousie had observed Lili and could point out ways for making changes to the book. She needed to be specific about what she was going to say and have time to talk.

Having settled down and chatted briefly, Firdousie introduced what she wanted to talk about. Practitioners complain that positive remarks, very often given at the beginning, can seem like a ploy before the 'bad' news comes. These need to be genuine and not just sweeteners or a way to avoid the main subject. Getting to the point early on helps to focus the discussion. It also avoids going off track while the person on the receiving end becomes nervous or irritated. Firdousie described the situation as she saw it; Lili, I notice . . . Using 'I' statements, such as I think, I see, shows that this is your point of view, how you see it. You want to describe the problem as you see it not label the person. In this case, Firdousie was concerned but not angry or upset with Lili. But sometimes you may have to express how you feel about something that has gone wrong or is not up to standard. Again, using 'I' : I find it difficult when . . .; I feel angry about . . . avoids labelling or blaming and is a statement of how you see the situation and feel about it.

CASE STUDY *continued*

Firdousie needed to be specific, not judgmental. She described the problem: Lili was writing too much so that the information was not easy for adults or children to access. She knew that Lili's first language was not English and did not focus on the grammar and spelling at this point but on the fact that these books were a shared resource for children and adults. She encouraged Lili to come up with ideas and introduced her to some strategies for changing the way she wrote these up with the children. Lili agreed to try these out.

At the end of the discussion, you may want to summarise what has been said. Just as it is important to start off well, so it is also important to make a definite ending and a positive one, if possible. You may arrange to meet again or thank the person for meeting with you. Both parties may feel uncomfortable at the end especially when there have been differences of opinion. At this point you both need time to yourselves, so moving on to another space or activity is better than hovering round each other. You will find a summary of giving critical feedback in Appendix 3 on page 119.

Giving and receiving praise

Most practitioners do not doubt that praising children is an important part of their interaction. But many find it difficult to receive or give it to other adults and deny or denigrate themselves when they hear it – *it was nothing; I just do it*. Some of this denial comes from cultural mores or habits people have grown up with: beliefs that saying what they can do or accepting compliments is a form of boasting or getting above oneself. But it is important that practitioners recognise their expertise and can be explicit about it, particularly when they work with other services, as we shall see in the next chapter. Like critical feedback, praise, if specific and straightforward, can give opportunities for people to think and reflect on what they have done. Making time to look back and talk about what has gone well before looking forward to what has to happen next gives practitioners the opportunity to acknowledge success and their part in it.

Labels such as *you're great, wonderful* may encourage but can become clichéd and are often not taken seriously. You will want to acknowledge when members of the team have achieved individually or together. Again if you use 'I', the person receiving the compliment focuses and hears it not as a general comment but a specific statement. For example, statements: *I liked the way you . . .*, or *I think it really worked well when you . . .* specifies what has actually been achieved. By acknowledging success and giving praise about particular ideas or practice, you create opportunities to think together about why something worked well and how you can move forward. It is easy to beat yourself up with all the things that have not gone right and not acknowledge what you have done. Listening to praise carefully yourself is also important. Accept it gracefully and remember it in the times when the going gets tough.

> *REFLECTIVE TASK*
>
> *Considering the ways to give critical feedback, how would you prepare and discuss changes with:*
>
> - *someone in the team who is excellent at her job but undervalues herself and therefore never puts herself forward to take on new opportunities;*
>
> - *someone in the team who is reluctant to change the way you work together and does not take your position in the team seriously?*

C H A P T E R   S U M M A R Y

This chapter has focused on the inevitability of change and how you can help yourself and others through the process. Your responsibility to innovate and share collective responsibility in implementing change (S35) requires an understanding of where conflicts may arise and how you bring these into the open and use them as ways to move forward. As an EYP, you may well be criticised. This can be painful or upsetting and we have suggested some ways of dealing with this assertively. We have also looked at ways of giving critical feedback and praise to others, suggesting that this is an important part of learning together.

Moving on

This chapter ended by suggesting that practitioners need to be explicit about their skills. This is particularly important when working with other services. In previous chapters, we have looked at some of the ways of developing effective teamwork and collaboration but mainly focused on what you would describe as your 'core' team. In the next chapter, we look at how this translates within a larger framework of multi-agency teams.

Self-assessment exercise

1 Change for me

What changes have you experienced in your work during the last year? Your examples may include changes in staff, children and parents, funding, procedures, physical reorganisation, or be more personal such as taking on more responsibility or changing your role.

Change	Losses	Gains

What I learnt about the process of change:

2 Supporting others through change

Consider the changes you have to make in your team. Think about the losses and gains for you and for others and then what support you can give as you go through the change process.

Change we have to make in the team	Losses/gains for me	Losses/gains for others	Support I can give through the process

FURTHER READING

Part 2 of Anning, A, Cottrell, D, Frost, N, Green, J, Robinson, M (2006) *Developing multiprofessional teamwork for integrated children's services: research, policy and practice*. Maidenhead: Open University Press.

8 Taking part in a multi-agency team

The Guidance to the Standards (CWDC, 2008a, page 67) states that if there is a multidisciplinary team within the setting then the EYP needs to *understand the extent, including limits, of their role and the expectations they should have of colleagues*. In earlier chapters the focus has been on your 'core' team but in this chapter, we ask you to take a wider view. Standard S36 uses the words *multiprofessional*, but in this chapter we use the term *multi-agency* and pick up some of the themes considered previously about working in a team, seeing them within a broader and national context. The chapter looks at the effects of legislation on multi-agency work and the way this translates into practice. It considers your role in a multi-agency team, suggesting that despite the complex issues for creating a universal service, your individual contribution is crucial in developing effective teams in your locality. It pays particular attention to the way different services share information to support children and their families.

After reading this chapter, you should be able to:
- discuss the factors that may help or hinder developing a multi-agency team;
- compare your role and responsibilities to other practitioners in a multi-agency team;
- identify some ways of sharing information with other services and with parents;
- understand the requirements of confidentiality when working in a multi-agency team.

The chapter has particular relevance to standard S36 but also refers to S33–S35. It considers your relationships with parents (S29–32) and suggests that working in a multi-agency team will require you to reflect on your own professional development (S39).

Introduction

The CWDC (2007b) describes multi-agency working as *ensuring the child only tells their story once*. Since the beginning of this century, putting the welfare of children and their families as a priority through integrated services has been enshrined in law. There has been a swathe of documents setting out government guidance and advice for developing a multi-agency approach, and much of the literature also highlights the challenges and dilemmas. This reflects the complexity of putting the policy into practice. It is easy to become overwhelmed by the huge changes that need to be put in place and disillusioned by the kind of publicity – such as the case of Baby P in 2008 – that tarnishes the reputation of others who are working together successfully. However, individual practitioners who work with other services usually display a real enthusiasm for doing so and are also realistic about the barriers they may have to overcome.

> **CASE STUDY**
>
> *Dee originally worked for a Traveller Education Project before joining a children's centre. She says that studying for a foundation degree, completing the NPQICL and her new role as manager has affected her practice but her essential beliefs remain the same:*
>
> > I always had to get on with people but I relied on their goodwill. Sometimes I had to 'sweet talk' different services into giving funds, working closely with the families, and sometimes, just taking them seriously. Now I can say you should be doing this. It's part of our work together. There are still stumbling blocks and some people feel threatened but I think there is more acknowledgment of what those working on the outskirts do, such as voluntary and specialist services.
>
> *Peggy, at a private nursery, although still not feeling an integral part of a universal service, says, nevertheless, that there is more support:*
>
> > Ten years ago I would have been petrified to ring up for help, partly I didn't know if I could and partly there weren't people out there. Now I have much more confidence that they will respond.

Working together

Pugh (2007) reminds us that there has always been a history of services working together. At the beginning of the twentieth century, for instance, the McMillan sisters recognised the importance of combined care and education; during the 1970s and 1980s, some joint social service and education nursery centres were set up. Community schools, largely developed in the 1970s, saw themselves as a resource in the community, staying open in the evening and offering adult education and group activities. Many Early Years settings have always made contact and developed close working relationships with health visitors, social workers and other services.

Worsley (2007, page 137) suggests that since there are few models for setting up and developing joined-up services, it is left to practitioners themselves to find new ways to work together and translate the policy into practice. Bertram *et al* (2002, page 10) in their report on early excellence centres found that the settings' shape and their *individualized nature* developed as a result of families' and individual's needs. Atkinson *et al* (2005) in their study of inter-agency groups, including education, health and social services in local authorities, found many models of joint working that are rarely evidenced in the literature. They also observed a *hybrid* professional, someone *who has personal experience and knowledge of other agencies, including importantly, understanding these services' cultures, structures, discourses and priorities* (Atkinson *et al*, 2005, page 16). They suggest that this would seem to be a *vital sine qua non for successful interagency collaboration*

(Atkinson *et al*, 2005, page 16) and that initial training and continuous professional development should include more cross-fertilisation of ideas.

REFLECTIVE TASK

- *How do you see your role in a multi-agency service?*

- *Which key people do you work with either directly or peripherally?*

- *Come up with two or three ideas for developing the sort of working relationship with other services that benefits children and their families.*

What is multi-agency working?

Sanders (2004, page 182) suggests that *joined-up thinking* is such a key part of government philosophy that the words may be taken for granted but that actually putting it into practice needs an *eyes wide open* approach. Certainly there is a profusion of terms used to discuss services working together and many attempts to define it. Jones (2008, page 127) refers to the following terms: *collaboration, partnership working, joined-up thinking and seamless thinking*. Lumsden (2005) argues that when practitioners work collaboratively, they do so at different levels and need to understand the different terminology to describe their work. She cites the work of Lloyd *et al* (2001) who define the various ways of working with the following terminology.

- *Inter-agency working: when more than one agency work together in a planned and formal way.*

- *Joined-up working: deliberate and co-ordinated planning and working which take account of different policies and varying agency practices and values. This can refer to thinking or to practice or policy development.*

- *Joint working: professionals from more than one agency working directly together on a project, for example, teachers and social work staff offering joint group work. School-based inter-agency meetings may involve joint planning, which reflects joined-up thinking.*

- *Multi-agency working: more than one agency working with a young person, with a family or on a project (but not necessarily jointly). It may be concurrent, sometimes as result of joint planning or it may be sequential.*

- *Single-agency working: where only one agency is involved this may still be the consequence of inter-agency decision making and therefore may be part of a joined-up plan.*

- *Multiprofessional working: the working together of staff with different professional backgrounds and training.*

- *Inter-agency communication: information sharing between agencies – formal and informal, written or oral.*

There are different interpretations of *multiprofessionalism*, where people work together but retain their traditional roles and specialisms, and interprofessionalism, where there is a greater willingness to share the knowledge for the benefit of those they are working with. Distinctions are also made between *inter* and *intra*, with the idea of *intra* expressing much closer links and shared responsibilities (Colloby, 2009).

REFLECTIVE TASK

- *Read Lloyd et al's terminology and reflect on the kind of terminology used in your area.*

- *Using Lloyd et al's categories, where would you place yourself and the work you do with other services?*

- *Consider where your setting is most successful in working with a variety of professionals and/or services. What do you think are the reasons for this?*

Why work together?

At the heart of the government's agenda is the well-being of children. *Every Child Matters* (DfES, 2003) was a response to Lord Laming's inquiry into the death of Victoria Climbié. It highlighted the need for services to intervene before children reached crisis point and ensure that children and families did not fall through the net when several agencies were involved with them. Thus a major area of the government agenda is the eradication of *the gross failure* of systems and *organisational malaise* (Laming, 2003, page 4) with a focus on child protection. The outcomes in *Every Child Matters* were given legal force in the Children Act 2004. With a holistic view of children and their families, childhood is seen as a continuous process, and co-operation between services supports this idea. Shifting the focus onto a child- and family-centred approach is most significant, suggests French (2007), because identifying outcomes means that specific questions can be asked when services are not delivering. To be able to monitor these outcomes, a range of services has to be involved and therefore also work together.

The DCSF describes anyone employed or volunteering with children and families as within a *children's workforce*, bringing together those working directly with children and those who may be working only with adults if they have children, such as a probation officer. The strategic responsibility for multi-agency work lies with the local authority and the DfES guidance (2005c, page 7) highlights the need for clear leadership and a *strong integrated governing board or structure representing all key delivery partners at senior level*. The way government departments and local authority services come together has far-reaching consequences for those on the ground. It is their responsibility to maintain standards and accountability and drive through the process. A major change has been the setting up of children's trusts with a director of children's services with responsibility for education, social services and health and for inter-agency co-operation. Moving from the separate directors for social services and education has meant making a cultural shift, and the leadership can bring to the fore differences in interpretation. For example, practitioners working with parents recognise a tension between two different agendas for *parenting* and *parent engagement*, emanating from government policy. Parenting programmes can imply they are for 'dysfunctional' families. Parent engagement is a more universal approach with the implication of partnership in children's education.

As well as shifting the focus on outcomes for the well-being of children and families, the Labour government also has an ambitious programme to eradicate child poverty by 2020. This has meant the input of massive funds to provide a range of services that span the whole family's needs with an expansion of childcare and family support but a focus also on employment for parents. Easily available resources are seen as a way of meeting the needs of *hard to reach* families and those who risk falling into the poverty trap. The Childcare Act (2006) puts the onus on local authorities to make sure the Every Child Matters agenda is implemented through the development of integrated services, notably through the development of Sure Start children's centres. This is an enormous challenge suggests Hoyle (2008, page 14) and can *gloss over* the much deeper inequalities in society, that arise from *structural and systemic problems*.

A UNICEF report (2007, Section 1.7) on child poverty in 21 industrialised nations based its research on six other dimensions as well as family income: material well-being, health and safety, education, peer and family relationships, behaviours and risks, and young people's own subjective sense of well-being. The UK was in the bottom third for five of these rankings with the exception of health and safety. While, recognising *Every Child Matters,* as a *sweeping vision about children's and young people's entitlements*, Hoyle is critical of central government driving the *grand vision*, but expecting local council services to put these into practice (Hoyle, 2008, page 13). Outreach workers in Early Years have always experienced the dilemma of encouraging parents to take full advantage of the educational opportunities offered when other issues, such as paying the rent or finding suitable housing have been at the top of their agendas. A family in poor housing is likely to suffer poor health and this may affect their children's education. Families where services are co-ordinated and resources are available may fare better than others.

CASE STUDY

Leila, a family support worker and the health visitor were visiting a family, under great stress, living in very poor accommodation with two-year-old twins and a baby on the way. Leila had developed excellent contacts locally and set up a multi-agency meeting, persuading the parents to become involved in the Common Assessment Framework, a process that can take an overall view of a family's circumstances. Through this consultation, she arranged additional sessions at the local nursery for the twins, and a practitioner in another service made contact with a housing association. As a result they agreed to find more suitable accommodation for the family.

Service level agreements

The government's expectation is that:

> All agencies work to prevent children suffering harm and to promote their welfare, provide them with the services they require to address their identified needs, and safeguard children who are being, or who are likely to be, harmed.
>
> *(Department of Health, 2004, page 17)*

McCullough (2007, page 35) describes two local authorities working in very different ways, one where the *higher echelons* were committed to integrated working in practice and the other where the culture of integrated working had not permeated the services. She contrasts the way the service level agreements were interpreted. In one, Health Services worked closely with Sure Start to ensure preventative measures and individual practitioners' work was significant in forging good relationships across services. But in the other, there was still a culture of dependency on certain services. The child protection team, under tremendous pressure, found that all agencies and other social service departments referred even minor issues, that they could have dealt with themselves, to them. Their fear was that because they were inundated with these, their team might *miss a real cause for concern* (McCullough, 2007, page 36).

CASE STUDY

1 *Lucy's experience of service agreements in her authority exemplifies the change of attitudes needed to bring about real integrated working. She says:*

   One of the big stumbling blocks is true information sharing. I think there is still a feeling that the information is so confidential that it can't be shared. Our centre has been here for five years and I discovered that a social worker had been working with a family on a child protection order close by. I feel we could give support to that family but the social worker didn't suggest it. She didn't seem to see the value of what we could offer.

2 *In contrast, Sam has helped build up a team around the children where she works and believes she and her immediate team are an integral part of a preventative service:*

   I did a lot of investing in getting to know who was out there previously but now I don't have to pester and services ring me up. The restructuring in the primary care trust has made a difference. We put on a dedicated health day every week at our centre, and the midwife, health visitor and child psychologist all come in on that day. It has made it so easy for parents in the community and they get to know what is on offer. It also makes referring parents to services very easy. I feel part of a really big team. We have even included the health workers' photos in our poster at the entrance. I also carry out some child development classes for teenage mothers at the local centre and then they find it easy to come to us. We organise a community day each year when people like the police, fire services, dental nurse and dietician all come in. They are now asking me when the next one will be.

Your role working in a multi-agency service

Multi-agency working is a central theme of the EYFS. The Common Core's expectations for multi-agency working is for practitioners *to work in a team context . . . respecting the contribution of others working with children, young people and families* (DfES, 2005a, page 18). In their research, Anning *et al* (2006) found that changing roles could take away practitioners' confidence; they give examples of a health visitor, nurse and special needs nursery nurse, who found moving from a specialist service to a mainstream one extremely painful. The guidance for multi-agency working (DfES, 2007a, page 2) acknowledges the overall challenges but emphasises the individual practitioner's contribution in putting the policy into practice:

> *. . . it is what happens at the interface between service providers and service users that is critical; in other words what happens on the ground as children and families go about their lives encountering different professionals for any number of reasons.*

This is certainly the starting point for you as an EYP driving forward agreed programmes (S36) and using many of the skills discussed in earlier chapters for developing an effective team. As Sam above shows, your contribution as an individual can impact on a multi-agency service as you speak up for children and families and offer and encourage high-quality practice in your setting. You will need to recognise and acknowledge your own particular expertise and knowledge and make this explicit (Edwards, 2004). This means recognising yourself as a resource with expertise that complements others' and building on this so that you and others can take advantage of being part of a service where there is a wealth of expertise and not *deskilled, all-purpose multi-agency* practitioners (Edwards, 2004, page 4).

CASE STUDY

Judy, leading on the community work in her setting, has found working in a multi-agency team particularly challenging and has noticed the rivalries within the team and the difficulty some practitioners have in giving up their status. The different work culture impacts on the practice. For example, on the one hand, she recognises and sympathises with the team of health visitors who are presently demoralised and preoccupied by the enormous workload they have to carry. On the other hand, she finds this frustrating because their communication systems are complicated and bureaucratic. Nevertheless she also feels that working in the team has expanded her horizons, and she has discovered new skills and gained new knowledge and experience. Working closely with a social worker has given her a much greater understanding of vulnerable families and issues around child protection.

Collaborating and communicating as a member of a multi-agency team

Before moving on to the challenges and dilemmas that dominate the main discourses, we will look now at some of the ways you can help to support collaborative teamwork and effective communication.

Filling the gaps and not duplicating services

A multi-agency approach requires services to look holistically at children's and families' needs. But the range of services and what they offer can be bewildering and over-whelming not just to practitioners, new to the work or a neighbourhood, but to parents too. Edwards (2004) refers to one study showing a child in contact with 50 different agencies in one local authority. Parents with children with special needs are particularly susceptible to having to deal with a huge number of people.

REFLECTIVE TASK

You may like to do this exercise with your team to exemplify the importance of knowing who is working or has worked with the families they are involved with.

- *Consider a family whose child may have special needs or whose children may have been in trouble at some time. List all those professionals that a family might come in contact with from the time a child is born to the time the child leaves school. You may want to start with the midwife.*

- *If you do this with your team, it is best to do it actively. Ask someone to stand in the middle to represent the family and then as others call a name out to come and stand next to them. You can ask them to place themselves close to the family if they think they are particularly important to the family or further out if they are not so involved. You may find there is a good deal of discussion about this placing.*

- *Discuss with the 'family' how it feels to be surrounded by these 'professionals' and ask for reactions from others.*

- *Consider the kind of information you give to parents about services in the neighbourhood, how easily they can access this and how you keep it up to date.*

This exercise, when actively carried out, clearly illustrates the pressures and confusion families may feel with the huge number of people surrounding them, possibly giving them very different advice. In one training session, with a large number of people, 'members of the extended family' who would also have an influence were included. As more and more people surrounded the 'family' and jostled for places, the 'family' retreated to the back of the room.

Understanding what other practitioners offer and supporting them

Anning *et al* (2006) and Powell (2007) suggest that recognising and discussing different perceptions of the child is an important part of multi-agency work. The health visitor, for instance, *might primarily view a child as a medical construction living within a social context, while a teacher might view the same child as an educational construction operating within a different social context* (Powell, 2007, page 25). This does not mean that either is incorrect, but both need to understand where the other stands; differing views can be beneficial for a child, so that he or she is not stereotyped. It can also engender a more creative approach to any support offered. Edwards (2004) highlights the need for recognising and respecting different approaches and making the effort to understand these.

CASE STUDY

Georgia describes how she changed her opinion of the speech therapist's practice when they were working together with a particular child:

> *I was surprised at how little the speech therapist said to the child and was critical at first. But as I worked with her more, I learnt from her about observing the small things, what I call the Scooby Doo effect. That is, standing back and watching, using and responding with non-verbal cues. My training had focused so much on children becoming verbal; hers had been much more about communication. I think you can get so set in your practice. Working with others definitely helps me to be more creative in my approach.*

REFLECTIVE TASK

- *Consider what knowledge and expertise you bring to a multi-agency team.*

- *What have you learnt, or how do you think you could develop your learning, by working with others who come from another service?*

- *What do you think are the best ways of combining your knowledge and expertise?*

Developing a shared vision with others

You looked at the importance of developing a clear vision with your 'core' teams and how this can be interpreted in different ways. Coming to an understanding of why you are working with other services is easier than actually putting this into practice. The legislation (Children Act, 2004) is the driving force behind services working together with a strong vision and belief that children can obtain the five outcomes of *Every Child Matters* and that these are a key to their well-being. The guidance suggests that the vision is a *unifying force*, helping people to focus on their roles and responsibilities (**www.everychild matters.gov.uk/deliveringservices/multiagencyworking/managerstoolkit**). Certainly, knowing that you are all working towards the same outcomes is helpful. It is how you interpret these that determine whether your work together is effective or not.

REFLECTIVE TASK

How do you see your role in achieving the five outcomes? Choose one of the following outcomes for children:

- *be healthy;*

- *stay safe;*

- *enjoy and achieve;*

- *make a positive contribution;*

- *promote good outcomes for children.*

Then consider how your role complements that of another practitioner in a multi-agency service in achieving this outcome.

Making the most of resources

You may be one of the fortunate ones in a setting where there is space, adequate materials and staffing. Dee is not so fortunate but describes how developing goodwill between services has paid off. *Doing a deal* with Homestart has meant that they offer a free counselling service for parents and she offers them a meeting room in her centre. The links with other services can extend outwards to those not immediately linked with you. Many Early Years practitioners make links with their local farms, museums or arts facilities, not only for the benefit of the children and families, but also to expand and rethink their own practice.

CASE STUDY

A group of six Early Years practitioners and six theatre practitioners met up for training together during several months, sometimes spending time away together. Maggie found it enhanced and changed her practice with the children:

> *I learnt to play more. We had to take the actors' place and perform, role play and it made me feel much more confident. When we joined together and made up stories with the children, some of the other staff found it odd and wanted to know what was the learning intention. I began to look at the children with a different eye and saw how much depth was coming out of the play. The actors who were with us learnt so much about children and realised they pitched things at too low a level when they performed for the children. The children don't need to be told all the time. They join in if they are interested. When I first joined the project with the actors, it all seemed a bit disorganised, but I feel much braver about being creative and take more risks now.*

Taking opportunities to find out about different values and cultures in other services

You have considered in earlier chapters the need to understand cultural barriers in other services. Boddy *et al*'s (2007) small study demonstrated how changes occurred in Early Years practitioners' and parents' attitudes after working closely with a link social worker placed in two children's centres. Most parents and practitioners regarded social services as a last resort or for those who have 'failed'. The change in this perception was mainly due to the visibility of the social worker who attended regular staff meetings, and spent time in the nursery and in stay and play sessions. The link social worker described the work as challenging and time-consuming, but believed it helped to *encourage a child-centred and outcome-focused approach to early intervention with families* (Boddy et al, 2007, page 2). Practitioners and parents felt much more at ease. At the same time, some practitioners felt there was an incompatibility when one person took on the role of individual caseworker and community social work. Having a day-to-day knowledge of families, as a community social worker was an advantage; however also having the role as a 'traditional' caseworker role within the centre was more complicated. Practitioners felt that the nature of the work demanded a different kind of relationship with families. Families might stop coming to children's centres to avoid the social worker. This could jeopardise practitioners' relationships with them and exclude some of the support they could offer them.

REFLECTIVE TASK

- *Do you agree with the practitioners' views above?*

- *How do you think different values and cultures can affect a joint service for children and families, positively or negatively?*

Sharing information

Who you share information with and how you do this is probably one of the greatest challenges for working in a multi-agency service. Do you and your team, as the Common Core puts it: *know who to share information with and when; understand the difference between information sharing on individual, organisational and professional levels* (DfES, 2005a page 22)? The guidance on sharing information emphasises the importance of personal information being kept safe and secure and that practitioners *maintain the privacy of the individual, whilst sharing information to deliver better services*. Members of your team need to be aware of the Human Rights Act and the Data Protection Act and it could be useful to have a discussion about what confidentiality involves. Legally, information can be shared if:

- it is not confidential in nature;
- the person to whom the duty is owed has given explicit consent;
- there is an overriding public interest in disclosure; or
- sharing is required by a court order or other legal obligation.

(DfES, 2006b, page 3)

and team members need to be clear of the implication of this for themselves, and for children and their families.

Powell (2007, page 26) suggests that what may appear uncomplicated in interprofessional communication *at closer examination reveals a sense of complexity*. For example, ContactPoint, an online directory with details of every child's name and address and a unique number to identify him or her was launched in January 2009 as a *quick way* (DCSF, 2009) for practitioners to find other services working with families. It is intended to *make it easier to deliver more coordinated support* and underpins the Children Act 2004, which puts a duty on children's services to co-operate to *improve the well-being of children* (Section 10) and *safeguard and promote the welfare of all children* (Section 11) (**www.everychildmatters.gov.uk/deliveringservices/contactpoint/**).

Convincing practitioners that this is a good way of holding information may take some time however.

J: *I was one of the 25 million whose child benefit records went missing when those computer discs were lost. I don't know how keen parents will be on having their names on yet another database.*

A: *There's a different method for health records. That's not going to make it easy.*

J: *Well, we'll wait and see. It won't take the place of talking to each other will it?*

Several different opinions were expressed when ContactPoint was launched, reflecting some of the practitioners' concerns (Shepherd, 2009): some civil liberties groups worry about its potential for abuse. The Association of Directors of Children's Services (ADCS) had expressed *significant* concerns before its introduction. Barnardo's chief executive's view, however, was that it could create a better service and more co-ordination if used by authorised professionals. Lord Laming, from whose report the importance of sharing information originates, called ContactPoint a useful tool but stressed the need for services to still work effectively across teams (Shepherd, 2009). His use of the word *tool* is perhaps significant, and this debate illustrates the complexity of sharing information and also the care that services must take to do this.

What are your views on having a national database? How do you see its usefulness and do you have any concerns about the increased ease with which information can be transmitted?

The Common Assessment Framework

The Common Assessment Framework (CAF) was introduced to provide a process for practitioners to exchange information so families would not have to repeat their story to several services. If you are not already familiar with the CAF, you can find it and guidance on how to use it at **www.everychildmatters.gov.uk/resources-and-practice/IG00063/**. There is also general guidance, regularly updated, for practitioners and managers, at the *Every Child Matters* site (**www.everychildmatters.gov.uk**). This includes an Information Sharing Vision Statement (2008, **www.everychildmatters.gov.uk/resources-and-practice/IG00340/**), the Children's Plan (2007, **www.dcsf.gov.uk/childrensplan/**) and the Think Family reports (2006, 2008, **www.cabinetoffice.gov.uk/social_exclusion_task_force/publications.aspx**). The CAF is intended to be a framework to follow and provides a common format for sharing information about children with additional needs where it is considered they may need extra support to achieve the five *Every Child Matters* outcomes. It is holistic in its approach and child centred, and considers three themes:

* the child's development;
* parents and carers;
* family and environment.

Its main aim is to provide a way of building on information that is already available, thus offering a more cohesive approach to parents.

CASE STUDY

Sarah is a member of a local authority language and communication team and works closely with a speech and language therapy service, educational psychologists, social services and a child development team. Working with children with complex needs, members of this team have been working together for six years and people are clear about their roles but they found that the CAF, as laid out, did not work for them and they have adapted it.

Sam, on the other hand, has found the CAF invaluable for sharing information with her multi-agency team and they have not changed the layout at all.

Sarah's and Sam's teams may carry out the assessment slightly differently but both reflect the steps in the CAF:

- prepare;

- discuss;

- deliver.

Parental engagement in the process and their co-operation is crucial if the information is to be helpful to them. Assuming that all parents will be willing to have their child's life discussed and recorded is simplistic, suggests Jones (2008), and this may be the reason that some practitioners are reticent about involving them. Brandon *et al* (2006) found that a considerable percentage of parents were not shown the CAF. Sharing information about children with other agencies is also complex and, as Jones (2008) recommends, practitioners need to be aware of confidentiality issues within the Data Protection Act 1998 and also know when it is possible to pass on information without consent. Brandon *et al*'s research (2006, page 50) found that parents appreciated a *friendly, informal manner* and relating to one person, but they stress that within this informality there needs to be a formality that follows the guidelines. Otherwise parents are not always sure about the process or, indeed, what they are giving their consent to. They found examples of experienced and qualified practitioners and some *charismatic* ones without qualifications who were able to combine the informal and formal approach, involving parents in completing the CAF form and also keeping them up to date with the proceedings. In their research in Scotland, Lloyd *et al* (2001) explored the involvement of parents and older children in decision-making about school exclusion. They found that although the three local authorities researched all had policies to involve parents, only one actually invited parents to the inter-agency school-based meetings. The other two invited parents to subgroup meetings with particular staff. Parents who attended the full meetings, however, valued being invited although they could sometimes find it intimidating and did not always understand what was being discussed.

The lead professional

If, at the end of the CAF process, it appears that the child or family requires support from a number of services, then a lead professional will take on the role of co-ordinating this. The role of the lead professional is to:

- act as a single point of contact for the child or family;
- co-ordinate the delivery of the actions agreed;
- reduce overlap and inconsistency in the services received.

(CWDC, 2008b, page 1)

The role can be taken on by anyone who is appropriately informed or qualified. As the guidance states, the lead professional is likely to be different for a child with a disability or specific need such as speech and language from one where the focus is on the parents' needs, such as help with behaviour management or improving the mother's self-esteem. Brandon *et al* (2006) found the lead professional role worked best when there was a previous history of agencies working together and commitment at both grassroots and managerial level. Some practitioners were worried by the responsibility, but with good support, training and guidance, their anxieties usually diminished.

CASE STUDY

Sarah's team have found it awkward making the decision about who should be the lead professional when the parent or carer is present in the meeting because it could appear that no-one wanted to take responsibility. Team members could become anxious about being appointed, either because they felt the pressures of more work or felt unsure about what they would have to do. Sometimes the most logical person did not have the resources or time, particularly if they worked in the voluntary sector. They now spend time after the meeting choosing an appropriate person, and discussing this with the parent afterwards to make sure they are happy with the choice.

The idea of *holding the baton* for the child (McCullough, 2007) illustrates the idea of working as a team. The responsibility remains with the whole team but when you have the baton, you are responsible for liaising with others including the parents. You may pass the baton on if another agency becomes the most appropriate one to take on the responsibility. However, as in a relay race, it is imperative to pass this baton carefully and not to drop it in the process. It is also important that the parents are included in discussions and decisions.

REFLECTIVE TASK

- *What is your view on inviting parents to large inter-agency meetings? What do you think could help them to feel a valued member of the meeting?*
- *In your present role, what strengths do you feel you could bring to the role of lead professional?*
- *Are there any areas you feel you need further training or support in taking this role on?*

Working with parents in a team

We have mainly discussed teams comprising practitioners but we end this chapter by suggesting that parents also have a major part to play in teams, both as participants and as an influence on the purpose and principles. Powell (2007) emphasises the importance of the style in which practitioners engage with parents. Multi-agency teams were set up to support parents and give them information more coherently and comprehensively. But there is a danger that as services come together they develop a collective voice that becomes so powerful it blocks out the voices of the children and parents. As we pointed out earlier, parents can meet an enormous array of practitioners whose roles and responsibilities vary, and they need to be clear about the kind of relationship they have with them. A parent attending a CAF meeting may find the individual practitioner they relate to very different when seeing him or her in a group of other practitioners. The balance of power may change and this can be awkward for the practitioner and the parent.

Powell (2007), citing Foucault (1997, page 79), suggests that a top-down approach can mean that children and parents can be *trained correctly*, so that they see things in the same way as the practitioners. Klavins (2008), in her report on involving parents in self-evaluation processes, found the leaders recognised that parents were often reluctant to say anything negative. You saw in the last chapter the skills needed to do this assertively. When parents actually did say what they thought and their viewpoint was quite different, practitioners did not find this easy. But as the report suggests, by listening to parents on an individual and daily basis, practitioners can share very valuable information. How this information is used will depend on the individual but also on developing effective systems, particularly in large settings, so that the information reaches the relevant *decision making bodies* (Klavins, 2008, page 12).

As we have stressed throughout this book, multi-agency collaboration and communication are there to develop a service where children and families are respected and consulted. Atkinson *et al* (2005, page 13) identified some key factors for success in multi-agency work, placing them in this order:

- commitment or willingness to be involved;
- commitment at a strategic level 'bottom-up' and 'top down' approach;
- belief in multi-agency work;
- understanding roles and responsibilities;
- (also understanding the constraints on people – 'hybrid' professionals were those who had worked in a number of different agencies);
- common aims and objectives;
- communication and information sharing;
- leadership as strategic drive and tenacity that could surmount any obstacles to progress; and leadership as a strategic vision that could bring together the team required in order to effect change;
- involving the relevant personnel;
- sharing and access to funding and resources.

You will notice that their first factor is *commitment and willingness to be involved*. Jones (2008, page 128) too suggests that the success of multi-agency work in practice may well rest with the individual practitioners and *cooperation of those individuals implementing the policy in their settings*. It is a huge task to take on nationally, with many challenges, but you have to start somewhere and as an EYP you are in a position to do this. As you understand and make explicit your skills and experience, and through co-operation and collaboration, encourage others to do the same, you can play a significant part in making local services, at least, more relevant and accessible to families.

C H A P T E R   S U M M A R Y

This chapter has considered the complexity of developing a multi-agency service for all children and their families. It has looked at the government's rationale in driving this policy and at the local authorities' and their partners' roles in putting this into practice and being accountable. It has discussed how children's and parents' rights to confidentiality are respected as information sharing becomes increasingly data based. It has considered some of the barriers that have to be surmounted but emphasised the importance of recognising and making explicit what you as an individual can offer to parents and colleagues by encouraging collaboration and communication.

Self-assessment exercise

Consider the following:

Question	Evidence	Area for development
How knowledgeable am I about services in my neighbourhood?		
How well do I share this information with parents and other practitioners?		
What particular expertise and knowledge do I bring to a multi-agency team?		
How clear am I about the roles and responsibilities of practitioners in other services?		
What do I do to make sure agreed programmes are followed up and monitored?		
How clear am I about what confidentiality entails and ways of sharing information?		
What do I do to encourage a commitment to multiprofessional/multi-agency work in my immediate team?		

Klavins, L (2008) *Parents matter: how can leaders involve parents in the self-evaluation process and further development of children's centre and extended school services.* Research associate report. Nottingham: National College for School Leadership.

www.ncsl.org.uk/klavins-parents-matter-summary-2.pdf

Siraj-Blatchford, I, Clarke, J, Needham, M (eds) (2007) *The team around the child: multi-agency working in the early years.* Stoke-on-Trent: Trentham Books.

Appendix 1:
Practical task – Damaging meetings (page 69)

Below are some of the words the group came up with for this exercise:

- distracting
- disturbing
- disagreeing continually
- dominating
- damning with faint praise
- denigrating others
- divulging private information
- dividing
- deviating
- dozing
- defending and attacking
- digressing
- destroying confidence
- decrepitating (heating a substance till it cracks – getting back at someone)
- digging into a position
- demanding attention
- denying all knowledge
- dithering over decisions
- discussing in private
- disrupting
- droning on
- doubting
- directionless
- defeatism
- demoralising
- dictating
- dashing through
- data overload
- dismissing
- discriminatory

Appendix 2:
Action minutes

Meeting title: Date:

*Present: Apologies:

*Where someone is not present for the whole meeting mark the items they are there for by their name.

Agenda item	Item under discussion	Action	By whom	Deadline

Appendix 3: Giving critical feedback – a summary

With acknowledgement to Anne Dickson.

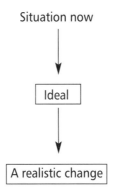

Situation now

↓

Ideal

↓

A realistic change

Giving constructive feedback to others can be helpful. It can change things. The feedback is helpful when it is based on an observable problem or behaviour. Before you begin, be clear in your mind, what changes you would like to see.

1 Choose a suitable time and place.

2 Explain the situation as you see it.

3 Describe the 'problem' or 'behaviour' without 'labelling' the person.

4 Use 'I' – i.e. *I find it difficult when* . . .

5 Be specific. Be descriptive rather than judgmental.

6 Express what you feel – e.g. *I feel annoyed; I feel disappointed*.

7 Say what you want to but acknowledge the other person's needs and feelings. Be careful you do not manipulate or allow yourself to be manipulated.

8 Give the other person an opportunity to give their view so the interaction is equal. They may not agree or may come back with criticism about you, so be prepared to respond to this.

9 Be clear about what you want to see finally.

10 Aim to end on a positive note – e.g. *I'm glad we've talked about this.*

11 Make a definite ending to the interaction.

Describing the situation without putting the other person down

- Describe the situation: *When . . .*

- Express your feelings without blame or judgment: *I feel . . .*

- Specify the change you would like: *I would prefer . . .; I would like . . .; I believe it would work better if . . .*

- Say what you see as the positive consequences: *If you do this, then . . .; If we do this . . .*

- If necessary, say what you see as the negative consequences: *If you don't . . .; If we're not able to . . .*

References

Adair, J (1987) *Effective teambuilding.* London: Pan.

Alberti, R, Emmons, M (2008) *Your perfect right: assertiveness and equality in your life and relationships*, 9th edition. Atascadero, CA: Impact Publishers.

Anning, A, Cottrell, D, Frost, N, Green, J, Robinson, M (2006) *Developing multiprofessional teamwork for integrated children's services: research, policy and practice.* Maidenhead. Open University Press.

Anning, A, Edwards, A (2006) *Promoting children's learning from birth to five: developing the new early years professional.* Maidenhead: Open University Press.

Anning, A (2001) *Knowing who I am and what I know: developing new versions of professional knowledge in integrated service settings.* Paper presented to the British Educational Research Association Annual Conference, University of Leeds, September 2001.

Atkinson, M, Doherty, P, Kinder, K (2005) Multi-agency working: models, challenges and key factors for success. *Journal of Early Childhood Research*, 3(1): 7–17.

Aubrey, C, David, T, Godfrey, R, Thompson, L (2000) *Early childhood educational research: issues in methodology and ethics.* London: Routledge/Falmer Press.

Back, K, Back, K (2005) *Assertiveness at work: a practical guide to handling awkward situations*, 3rd edition. Maidenhead: McGraw-Hill.

Belbin, M (1981) *Management teams: why they succeed or fail.* Oxford: Heinemann.

Bertram, T, Pascal, C (2002) *Early years education: an international perspective.* London: Qualifications and Curriculum Authority. **www.inca.org.uk** (accessed 7 April 2009).

Bertram, T, Pascal, C, Bokhari, S, Gasper, M, Holtermann, S (2002) *Early excellence centre pilot programme. Second evaluation report 2000–2001.* Research report 361. Nottingham: DfES.

Biggs, J (1996) *Teaching for quality learning at university.* Buckingham: Open University Press.

Boddy, J, Wigfall, V, Simon, A (2007) *Re-discovering community social work? An evaluation of a social worker based in children's centres.* **www.communitycare.co.uk/Articles/2007/06/14/104802/research-childrens-centre-pilot-link-worker-post.html** (accessed 7 April 2009).

Bolam, R, McMahon, A, Stoll, L *et al* (2005) *Creating and sustaining effective professional learning communities.* Research report 637. Bristol: University of Bristol.

Brandon, M, Howe, A, Dagley, V *et al* (2006) *Evaluating the common assessment framework and lead professional guidance and implementation in 2005–6.* Research report RR740. Nottingham: DfES. **www.dcsf.gov.uk/research/data/uploadfiles/RR740.pdf** (accessed 7 April 2009).

Brock, A (2006) *Dimensions of early years professionalism – attitudes versus competences?* **www.tactyc.org.uk/pdfs/Reflection_brock.pdf** (accessed 7 April 2009).

Cameron, C (2006) Men in the nursery revisited: issues of male workers and professionalism. *Contemporary Issues in Early Childhood*, 7(1): 68–79.

Chandler, T (2006) Working in multidisciplinary teams, in Pugh, G, Duffy, B (eds) *Contemporary issues in the early years*. London: Sage Publications.

Childcare Act 2006. London: HMSO. **www.opsi.gov.uk/acts/acts2006/pdf/ukpga_20060021_en.pdf** (accessed 17 April 2009).

Children Act 2004. London: HMSO. **www.opsi.gov.uk/Acts/acts2004/ukpga_20040031_en_1** (accessed 17 April 2009).

Children's Workforce Development Council (CWDC) (2007a) *Every child matters: change for children: multi-agency working*. **www.everychildmatters.gov.uk/_files/16BD8C63438670F6C07F6D5FF 5EAD178.pdf** (accessed 7 April 2009).

Childrens Workforce Development Council (CWDC) (2007b) *Integrated working*. **www.cwdcouncil. org.uk/integrated-working/storyonce**

Childrens Workforce Development Council (CWDC) (2008a) *Guidance to the award of early years professional*. Leeds: CWDC.

Children's Workforce Development Council (CWDC) (2008b) *The lead professional fact sheet*. **www.cwdcouncil.org.uk/lead-professional** (accessed 7 April 2009).

Clark, A, Moss, P (2001) *Listening to young children: the mosaic approach*. York: Joseph Rowntree Foundation Publications.

Coleman, M (2005) Organisations: power, structure and culture., in Coleman, M, Earley, P (eds) (2005) *Leadership and management in education: cultures, change and context*. Oxford: Oxford University Press.

Colloby, J (2009) *The validation process for EYPS*, 2nd edition. Exeter: Learning Matters.

Daly, M, Byers, E, Taylor, W (2004) *Early Years management in practice*. Oxford: Heinemann.

Darlington, Y, Feeney, JA, Rixon, K (2005) Practice challenges at the intersection of child protection and mental health. *Child and Family Social Work*, 10: 239–247.

Data Protection Act 1998. London: HMSO.

David, T (2007) Birth to three: the need for a loving and educated workforce, in Moyles, J (ed) *Early years foundations: meeting the challenge*. Buckingham: Open University Press.

Daycare Trust and TUC (2008) *Raising the bar: what next for the early childhood education and care workforce? Childcare futures: policy insight paper 1*. London: Daycare Trust. **www.daycaretrust. org.uk/mod/fileman/files/Raising_the_bar_Nov08.pdf** (accessed 20 April 2009).

DCSF (2008a) *2020 Children and young people's workforce strategy*. Nottingham: DCSF. **www.publications.teachernet.gov.uk/eOrderingDownload/7977-DCSF-2020%20 Children%20and%20Young%20People%27s%20Workforce%20Strategy-FINAL.pdf** (accessed 7 April 2009).

DCSF (2008b) *Statutory framework for the early years foundation stage: setting the standards for learning, development and care for children from birth to five*. Nottingham: DCSF. **www.nationalstrategies.standards.dcsf.gov.uk/earlyyears/eyfs** (accessed 7 April 2009).

DCSF (2008c). *Practice guidance for the early years foundation stage*. Nottingham: DCSF. **www.standards.dcsf.gov.uk/eyfs** (accessed 7 April 2009).

DCSF (2008d) *Principles into practice cards. The early years foundation stage*. Nottingham: DCSF.

DCSF (2009) Written ministerial statement, January 2009: *Safeguarding*. **www.everychildmatters. gov.uk/_files/DCSF_ContactPoint_WMS_26_Jan_09.pdf** (accessed 17 April 2009).

Delehant, A (2007) *Making meetings work: how to get started, get going, and get it done*. London: Sage Publications.

Department for Education and Skills (DfES) (2003) *Every child matters* (Green Paper). London: HMSO. **www.dcsf.gov.uk/consultations/downloadableDocs/EveryChildMatters.pdf** (accessed 7 April 2009).

Department for Education and Skills (DfES) (2004) *Every child matters: change for children*. Nottingham: DfES. **www.everychildmatters.gov.uk/_files/F9E3F941DC8D4580539EE4C743E9371D.pdf** (accessed 17 April 2009).

Department for Education and Skills (DfES) (2005a) *Common core of skills and knowledge for the children's workforce*. Nottingham: DfES. **www.everychildmatters.gov.uk/deliveringservices/ commoncore/** (accessed 7 April 2009).

Department for Education and Skills (DfES) (2005b) Children's workforce strategy: a strategy to build a world-class workforce for children and young people. Nottingham: DfES. **www.dcsf.gov.uk/ consultations/downloadableDocs/5958-DfES-ECM.pdf** (accessed 7 April 2009).

Department for Education and Skills (DfES) (2005c) *Statutory guidance to inter-agency co-operation to improve the well-being of children: children's trusts*. Nottingham: DfES. **www.everychildmatters. gov.uk/_files/1200903D4F3C1396021B70D7146FAFEA.pdf** (accessed 7 April 2009).

Department for Education and Skills (DfES) (2006a) *Children's workforce strategy: building a world-class workforce for children, young people and families. The Government's response to the consultation*. Nottingham: DfES.

Department of Education and Skills (DfES) (2006b) *Information sharing: further guidance on legal issues. Integrated working to improve outcomes for children and young people*. **www.ecm.gov.uk/ informationsharing** (accessed 7 April 2009).

Department for Education and Skills DfES (2007a) *Early years foundation stage. Effective practice: multi-agency working*. Nottingham: DfES. **www.standards.dfes.gov.uk/eyfs/resources/downloads/ 3_4b_ep.pdf** (accessed 7 April 2009).

Department for Education and Skills DfES (2007b) *Multi-agency services: toolkit for managers*. **www.everychildmatters.gov.uk/deliveringservices/multiagencyworking/managerstoolkit/** (accessed 7 April 2009).

Department of Health (2004) *Every child matters: change for children in health services*. London: DH Publications. **www.everychildmatters.gov.uk/publications/** (accessed 7 April 2009).

Dickson, A (1982) *A woman in your own right*. London: Quartet Books.

Duffy, B, Marshall, J (2007) Leadership in multi-agency work, in Siraj-Blatchford, I, Clarke, J, Needham, M (eds) *The team around the child: multi-agency working in the early years*. Stoke-on-Trent: Trentham Books.

Edgington, M (2004) *The foundation stage teacher in action*, 3rd edition. London: Paul Chapman Publishing.

Edwards, A (2004) *Multi-agency working for prevention for children and families: 'it's the biggest change since the introduction of the NHS'*. Keynote presentation. The National Evaluation of the Children's Fund. **www.ne-cf.org/conferences/home.asp?conferenceCode=00020008** (accessed 7 April 2009).

Eyles, J (2007) Vision, mission, method: challenges and issues in developing the role of the early years mentor teacher, Chapter 8, in Moyles, J (ed) (2007) *Early years foundations: meeting the challenge*. Maidenhead: Open University Press.

Foot, H, Howe, C, Cheyne, B, Terras, M, Rattray, C (2000) Pre-school education: parents' preferences, knowledge and expectations. *International Journal of Early Years Education*, 8(3): 189–204.

Foucault, M (1983) What is enlightenment? in Rabinow, P (ed.) *The Foucault Reader*. Harmondsworth, Penguin.

Foucault, M (1997) *Discipline and punish: the birth of prison*. London: Penguin.

French, J (2007) Multi-agency working: the historical background, in Siraj-Blatchford, I, Clarke, J, Needham, M (eds) (2007) *The team around the child: multi-agency working in the early years*. Stoke-on-Trent: Trentham Books.

Fullan, M (1991) *The new meaning of educational change*. London: Cassell.

Fumoto, H, Hargreaves, DJ, Maxwell, S (2004) The concept of teaching: a reappraisal. *Early Years: An International Journal of Research and Development*, 24(2): 179–191.

Gallagher, K, Rode, E, McClelland, B, Reynolds, J, Tombs, S (1997) *People in organisations: an active learning approach.* Oxford: Blackwell.

Garmston, RJ (2005) Group wise: no time for learning? Just take it in tiny bits and savor it. *Journal of Staff Development*, 26(4): 65.

Goldschmied, E, Jackson, S (2004) *People under three: young children in day care*, 2nd edition. London: Routledge.

Goleman, D (1996) *Emotional intelligence: why it can matter more than IQ.* London: Bloomsbury.

Grint, K (2005) Public opinion. *The Times*, 8 March. **www.business.timesonline.co.uk/tol/business/ industry_sectors/public_sector/article420933.ece** (accessed 7 April 2009).

Handy, C (1988) *Understanding voluntary organisations*. London: Penguin.

Handy, C (1990) *Inside organisations*. London: BBC Books.

Handy, C (1993) *Understanding organisations*, 4th edition. London: Penguin Books.

Hay, S (2008) *Essential nursery management: a practitioners guide*, 2nd edition. London: Nursery World/Routledge.

Hoag, B, Cooper, CL (2006) *Managing value-based organisations: it's not what you think.* Cheltenham: Edward Elgar Publishers Ltd.

Hoyle, D (2008) *Problematizing every child matters*. **www.infed.org/socialwork/every_child_ matters_a_critique.htm** (accessed 7 April 2009).

Janis, I (1972) *Victims of groupthink.* New York. Houghton Mifflin.

Jones, C (2008) Multi-agency working: rhetoric or reality? In Paige-Smith A, Craft, A, *Developing reflective practice in the early years.* Maidenhead: Open University Press.

Jones, C, Pound, L (2008) *Leadership and management in the early years.* Maidenhead: Open University Press.

Kinney, L (2005) Small voices . . . powerful messages, in Clark, A, Trine Kjørholt, A, Moss, P (eds) *Beyond listening: children's perspectives on early childhood services.* Bristol: The Policy Press.

Klavins, L (2008) *Parents matter: how can leaders involve parents in the self-evaluation process and further development of children's centre and extended school services.* Research associate report. Nottingham: National College for School Leadership.

Laevers, F (2005) The curriculum as means to raise the quality of early chldhood education: implications for policy. *European Early Childhood Education Research Journal*, 13(1): 17–29.

Laming, Lord H (2003) *The Victoria Climbié inquiry. Report of an inquiry by Lord Laming*, CM5730. London: The Stationery Office.

Lave, J, Wenger, E (1991) *Situated learning: legitimate peripheral participation.* Cambridge: Cambridge University Press.

Lewis Carroll, CD (1865) Chapter 5, in Alice's Adventures in Wonderland. **www.cs.indiana.edu/metastuff/wonder/ch5.html** (accessed 17 April 2009).

Lloyd, G, Stead, J, Kendrick, A (2001) *Inter-agency working to prevent school exclusion.* York: Joseph Rowntree Foundation. **www.jrf.org.uk/node/918** (accessed 7 April 2009).

Lumsden, E (2005) Joined up thinking in practice: an exploration of professional collaboration, in Waller, T (ed) *An introduction to early childhood.* London: Paul Chapman.

MacNaugton, G (2005) *Doing Foucault in early childhood studies: applying post-structural ideas.* London: Routledge.

McCall, C, Lawler, H (2000) *School leadership: leadership examined.* London: The Stationery Office.

McCullough, M (2007) Integrating children's services: the case for child protection, in Siraj-Blatchford, I, Clarke, J, Needham, M (eds) *The team around the child: multi-agency working in the early years.* Stoke-on-Trent: Trentham Books.

Mercer, N, Littleton, K (2007) *Dialogue and the development of children's thinking: a socio-cultural approach.* London: Routledge.

Miller, L (2008) Developing new professional roles in the early years, in Miller, L, Cable, C (eds) *Professionalism in the early years.* Abingdon: Hodder Education.

Morgan, G (1997) *Images of organization*, 2nd edition. London: Sage Publications.

Moss, P (2008) The democratic and reflective professional: rethinking and reforming the early years workforce, Chapter 11, in Miller, L, Cable, C (eds) *Professionalism in the early years.* Abingdon: Hodder Education.

Moss, P, Pence, A (eds) (1994) *Valuing quality in early childhood services: new approaches to defining quality.* London: Chapman.

Moyles, J (2001) Passion, paradox and professionalism in early childhood education. *Early Years: An International Journal of Research and Development*, 21(2): 81–95.

Moyles, J (2006) *Effective leadership and management in Early Years*. Maidenhead: Open University Press.

Moyles, J, Adams, S, Musgrove, A (2002) *SPEEL. The study of pedagogical effectiveness in early learning*. Research report 363. London: DfES.

National Chidminders Association (NCMA) (2006) *National childminding associations – NMCA*. **www.childrenwebmag.com/articles/child-care-articles/national-child-minding-associations-ncma**

Needham, M (2008) Keeping people in the big picture: national policy and local solutions, in Siraj-Blatchford, I, Clarke, J, Needham, M (eds) *The team around the child: multi-agency working in the early years.* Stoke-on-Trent: Trentham Books.

Neugabauer, R (1985) Are you an effective leader? *Child Care Information Exchange*, 46: 18–26.

Novinger, S, O'Brien, L (2003) Beyond 'boring, meaningless shit' in the academy: early childhood teacher educators under the regulatory gaze. *Contemporary Issues in Early Childhood*, 4(1): 4–18. **www.dx.doi.org/10.2304/ciec.2003.4.1.4** (accessed 17 April 2009).

Nutbrown, C (2006) *Threads of thinking: young children learning and the role of early education*, 3rd edition. London: Sage Publications.

Oberheumer, P (2005) Conceptualising the early childhood pedagogue: policy approaches and issues of professionalism. *European Early Childhood Education Research Journal*, 13(1): 5–16.

Osgood, J (2006) Deconstructing professionalism in early childhood education: resisting the regulatory gaze. *Contemporary Issues in Early Childhood*, 7(1): 5–14.

Osterman, K, Kottkamp, D (1993) *Reflective practice for educators: improving schooling through professional development.* Newbury Park: Corwin Press.

Pound, L (2008*)* Exploring leadership roles and responsibilities of the early years professional, in Paige-Smith, A, Craft, A (eds) *Developing reflective practice in the Early Years*. Maidenhead: Open University Press.

Powell, J (2007) Multi-agency development and issues of communication, in Nurse, A (ed) *The new Early Years professional: dilemmas and debates*. London: Routledge.

Pugh, G (2007) Foreword, in Siraj-Blatchford, I, Clarke, J, Needham, M (eds) *The team around the child: multi-agency working in the early years*. Stoke-on-Trent: Trentham Books.

Rinaldi, C (2006) *In dialogue with Reggio Emilia: listening, researching and learning.* London: Routledge.

Rodd, J (2006) *Leadership in early childhood*, 3rd edition. Maidenhead: Open University Press.

Rogoff, B (1990) *Apprenticeship in thinking: cognitive development in social context.* Oxford: Oxford University Press.

Sanders, B (2004) Inter-agency and multidisciplinary working, in Maynard, T, Thomas, N (eds) *An introduction to early childhood studies*. London: Sage Publications.

Schein, E (1992) *Organizational culture and leadership*, 2nd edition. San Francisco: Jossey-Bass.

Sharman, D (1993) *The perfect meeting: all you need to get it right first time*. London: Random House.

Shepherd, J (2009) New children's database faces criticism. *Guardian*, 26 January. **www.guardian.co.uk/society/2009/jan/26/childrens-database-contactpoint** (accessed 7 April 2009).

Siraj-Blatchford, I, Clarke, J, Needham, M (eds) (2007) *The team around the child: multi-agency working in the early years*. Stoke-on-Trent: Trentham Books.

Siraj-Blatchford, I, Manni, L (2006) *Effective leadership in the early years sector: the ELEYS study*. London: Institute of Education, University of London. **www.gtce.org.uk/shared/contentlibs/126795/93128/120213/eleys_study.pdf** (accessed 27 March 2009).

Siraj-Blatchford, I, Sylva, K, Muttock, S, Gilden, R, Bell, D (2002) *Researching effective pedagogy in the early years (REPEY)*. DfES research report 356. London: DfES.

Siraj-Blatchford, I, Sylva, K, Taggart, B, Melhuish, EC, Sammons, P, Eliot, K (2003) *The effective provision of pre-school education (EPPE) project (1997–2003)*. Technical paper 10: intensive case studies of practice across the foundation stage. London: DfES/Institute of Education, University of London.

Smith, A, Langston, A (1999) *Managing staff in early years settings*. London: Routledge.

Stoll, L (2004) *Leading communities: purposes, paradoxes and possibilities*. Professorial lecture. London: Institute of Education, University of London.

Southworth (1998) *Leading improving primary schools*. London: Falmer Press.

Sylva, K, Melhuish, EC, Sammons, P, Siraj-Blatchford, I, Taggart, B (2004) *The effective provision of pre-school education (EPPE) project: final report*. London: DfEE/Institute of Education, University of London.

Tropman JE (1996) *Effective meetings: improving group decision-making*, 2nd edition. London: Sage Publications.

Tuckman, B (1965) Developmental sequence in small groups. *Psychological Bulletin*, 63(6): 384–399.

Tuckman, B, Jensen, M (1977) Stages of small group development revisited. *Group and Organization Management*, 2: 419–427.

UNICEF (2007) *Child poverty in perspective: an overview of child well-being in rich countries*. Innocenti Report Card 7. Florence: UNICEF Innocenti Research Centre. **www.unicef.org.uk/publications/pub_detail.asp?pub_id=124** (accessed 7 April 2009).

Van Oers B, Hännikäinen M (2001) Some thoughts about togetherness: an introduction. *International Journal of Early Years Education*, 9(2): 101–108.

Vygotsky, L (1978) *Mind in society*. Cambridge, MA: Harvard University Press.

Wenger, E (1998) *Communities of practice: a brief introduction*. Cambridge: Cambridge University Press.

Whalley, ME (2008) *Leading practice in early years settings*. Exeter: Learning Matters.

Woodcock, M, Francis, D (1994) *Teambuilding strategy*, 2nd edition. Aldershot: Gower Publishing.

Worsley, J (2007) Exploring the perspectives of early years practitioners in a newly established children's centre, in Siraj-Blatchford, I, Clarke, J, Needham, M (eds) *The team around the child: multi-agency working in the early years*. Stoke-on-Trent: Trentham Books.

Index